POSTCARDS OF SEAGROVE

BY
GARRETT HORN

To Polly,

All the Best,

[signature]

First published in the United States of America in 2016 by
Garrett Horn Publishing, Seagrove, Florida.

ISBN 978-0692691410

Printed by CreateSpace.
Designed by Garrett Horn and Ginger Jackson Sinton.

DEDICATION

This book is dedicated to my father, Robert Horn; my mother, Rita Vreeland Horn; and to my siblings: Richard Horn, Barbara Horn Thaler, and William Horn, who have always been with me through the years. And most especially, this book is dedicated to my wife, Nina McCaslin Horn, who has been my inspiration for the greatest part of my life.

ACKNOWLEGMENTS

I want to thank the people who have helped create this book. I want to thank Ginger Jackson Sinton, most of all, for doing an excellent job as designer and editor. I, especially, want to thank Bill Horn, Didon Comer, Maunsel White, Flip Spann, Manny Chavez, and any others that may have contributed photography to this book. The front cover is a photograph of an oil painting by Mary Bryan Bruns, completed in the early fifties. This painting captures the essence of early Seagrove.

INTRODUCTION

Hampton Echoes believed he could write a book. Throughout his life, he seemed to think he was driven by some madman called fate to write the really true experiences of evolving through the latter half of the twentieth century, in the United States, on the earth, with the Universe. In scattered impulses he sketched down many of his ideas. Fragmented, demented, sometimes brilliant, often incoherent, these thoughts, at times, somehow became clear and valid even to me. But, I am not an unbiased observer, having gone through close to half a lifetime of grueling and beautiful friendship with him, and it is because I was the last person to see him before he mysteriously disappeared on the eve of 1984, that I am writing, or severely editing, this book. At times, I may lapse into the first person singular in certain passages but it comes from being truly close to Hamp's feelings. I assure you that I have no idea how his mind really works. The fact that he never really finished his book, but merely left a rather astonishing collection of notebooks, is what left me with the rather arduous task of organizing a nebulous cluster of facts and fantasies into comprehensible form. And yet, I have attempted at the same time to give an objective portrait of a young man I've known almost all my life. The following manuscript is my recollections of the times and mind of Hampton Echoes, an alias he took on later on, with many excerpts from his notebooks, all tied together with a bit of pipedream and love for my good friend.

Garrett Horn
February 22, 1984
Seagrove Beach

Introduction Too

Memories seem to me, to be like pieces of driftwood. They have been cast off into the ocean at a certain point in time. They have been swirled through all the storms, and have floated peacefully through every tranquil lull. And then they just appear one day along the shoreline of our thoughts, as we stroll along in our day-to-day with our deep thoughts and curiosities. These memories emerge, half buried in the sands, and they seem so smooth, so perfect in their twisted form. They appear almost polished by the years of time that have washed over them. These pieces are so precious, so fragile. We should always take the time to walk along the tide line and gather each and every piece of timeless treasure that washes our way. We should gather our memories and frame a picture, or perhaps, a mirror, to truly look and see ourselves, surrounded by our most precious treasures, our memories.

Hampton Echoes

"The difference between the right word and the almost right word is the difference between lightning and a lightning bug."

—*Mark Twain*

"An artist never finishes his work; he only abandons it."

—*somebody else*

"A canoe can be so silent. With a little caution, you can dip the paddles cleanly, quietly through the waters. You can venture over still, glassy lakes almost like a breeze...never disturbing the balance. And always remember...be careful...it's a garden out there..."

—*me*

FROM BAYOU TO BEACH CLUB

It was a family secret, in a way. It was a little meandering creek back behind Seagrove that nobody really knew about. My friend took me to explore it many years ago. We slipped our canoe into the stream and paddled through the dark silent waters, past the scrub oaks, the pine trees, and the palmettos. The creek twisted north and south as it ambled slowly west, with sawgrass reaching far overhead. Every turn brought a new breathtaking view of Florida backwaters. Once, we edged closer to what seemed to be a silent tree stump in the water, only to have it burst into noisy flutter as a blue heron soared into flight. We realized there was a multitude of wildlife surrounding us, hidden in this sanctuary. We watched the passing shores ever more closely, hoping to catch sight of an elusive deer or raccoon. A hawk circled sleepily overhead. Every so often, something broke the water. We hoped it was a big bass. There might be 'gators out here, we imagined. And yes, there probably were...

Our boat was my old trusty fourteen-foot patchwork Grumman canoe, but with a lot of imagination, we could have been Bogart and Hepburn on the African Queen. When the twisting "river" finally spilled into open water, it wasn't quite Lake Victoria, but it was about as breath-taking as a body of water could be. Since this first excursion happened on my birthday, I named it "Birthday Bayou". You won't find it on any map, but if you venture north from the center of WaterColor, you can't miss it. Slip off in your own little rowboat, embark on your own journey downstream, and, perhaps, discover a bayou no one has ever seen before.

Fast-forward about a dozen and a half years, and it's the Fourth of July, 2001. I found myself on the banks of Birthday Bayou, once more, and I'm still in the midst of discovery, in the new neighborhoods of WaterColor. My brother and I, and our girlfriends, are exploring the fantastic marina building nestled on the shore of Western Lake. Racks for canoes and kayaks are apparent as well as a boat-building shop. It takes no imagination at all to see what a unique, quaint building this will be. Up the hill, the timber frame of a special restaurant stood against the sky. We discovered a fabulous fun little treehouse built into the sugar pines. The ghosts of Tom Sawyer and Huckleberry Finn had to be nearby.

Upward and inland we ventured. We had heard talk of bridges, and everywhere we walked, we came across some new variation of them... long ones, short ones, curved ones, even a big one. There were small waterfalls, a gentle tile-lined aqueduct that bordered the central park, and a fascinating fishpond. Just "showfish," nothing we could take home for supper. Everywhere about were pine trees, scrub oaks, and palmetto, left just as they are, with new plantings of stuff I really didn't even need to know the names of. There were gravel paths lending a certain order to it all.

Then, we suddenly became aware of the music. There was jazz in the air, coming from somewhere south. We wandered towards it through the town center, window-peeked in the sales office, and kept heading toward the ocean. Between the shore and us was a large, colorful, bunch of buildings. A flight of steps invited us up into a yellow watchtower and a few steps later we emerged onto a pool, like nothing I had ever seen before. Sea oats swayed gently nearby, the glistening Gulf wrapped out to the horizon, and a pristine line of ancient sand dunes sheltered us back into the plaza of the pool. Natives seem to emerge from nowhere, offering us towels and festive cocktails. One more flight of stairs and we were perched on stainless steel barstools lined around the upstairs snack bar observatory. On one side, the town of Seaside looked even more storybook from this vantage. All in front of us, the Gulf of Mexico lay spread like a...umm...watercolor. Toward the west, Western Lake was waiting with more adventures, tomorrow. From bayou to beach club, discovering Northwest Florida had come a long way.

The Cottage At Eastern Lake

The year was '59. The number one song on the airwaves was "A Summer Place." My mom and dad, Rita and Robert Horn, piled Barbara, Rick, Bill, and myself into the '57 Chevy station wagon, took highway 331 south out of Selma one morning, and we ended up in Seagrove. It changed my life. I was seven years old. We stayed at some friends' cottage on the bluff in the middle of Seagrove. It didn't take my dad long to venture down some of the dirt roads and jeep tracks that led in various directions from there. In those days, there was no highway 30-A. The Seagrove Road led down from highway 98 to Russell's Grocery (which later became The Seagrove Village Market) and then, abruptly stopped. The beginnings of 30-A led west about half-way to Western Lake and eastward about the same distance. My dad headed east one day and, when the pavement ended, he took a winding little used jeep track that skirted the dunes, and ended up at an old cottage on Eastern Lake. The old shack was nestled in the scrub oaks and sat quietly on a bluff overlooking the gentle waters. Across the lake, the sand dunes spread out as far as the eye could see and the Gulf of Mexico lay glistening in the distance.

My dad instantly removed the For Sale sign from the fencepost, called the person selling the place, Billy Wesley, and assured him that we would never tamper with the nature of the place, we would solemnly protect the trees, and generally just keep things as they were. Before long, the cottage was our "summer place."

There is nothing as beautiful as an old Florida beach cottage. The cedar shingled roof, the concrete block screened porch, the pine siding with its peeling paint, the sand-worn wooden floors and the shiplap walls and ceilings; the sticky, wood double-hung windows held up with pieces of old dip-nets, chair legs, or pieces of driftwood; the faded linoleum kitchen floor with the round-topped Frigidaire, painted red, to hide the rust. Next to the sink stood the hand-pump that served as back-up when the power would go out. Often as not, on big holidays like the 4th of July, we would have a power outage and it would be necessary to pump a bucket of water and take it to the bathroom to flush the toilet. Most times we hardly needed the electricity anyway.

My dad spent his time tinkering with the sailboat he had designed and built himself. Mom mostly sunbathed. Fishing and catching crabs were the rule of the day for us kids. It was not uncommon to catch maybe fifty crabs on a good day. And I can remember at least one day when the count was nearly a hundred! Checking the traps twice a day for big blue crabs, then roaming the inlet and the seashore at sunset to catch calicos. At night we would boil them all, and pick them apart on the old cedar-log picnic table that doubled as the Ping-Pong table after dinner. After sailing and swimming and crabbing and fishing and beachcombing all day long in the hot summer sun, bedtime came early. No one ever forgot, though, no matter how tired we were, to complete the day's last ritual: sweeping the sand from your bed, to preserve a gentle resting place for your sunburnt skin.

I remember one summer, my friend Tommy and I both had injuries suffered in football spring training. Turtle, as he was called, had broken his right ankle and had a cast up to his knee. I had torn the ligaments in my left knee and had a cast from my ankle to my hip. We actually had a system where we could walk together, arm-in-arm, and not need our crutches. But it was summer! And it was hot. Everyone was walking to the beach and leaving us far behind, or going swimming in the Gulf, and we were bummed-out beach boys. Finally, we found a solution: We hobbled ourselves to the old wooden rowboat, rowed our way out to the middle of the lake, and took turns, awkwardly sticking our heads over the side and into the cool refreshing water. We did take a moment's pause to wonder what my mom was screaming about, at the top of her lungs, on the lakeshore; but we didn't let it bother us. Later, in no uncertain terms, she pointed out to us that if we had tipped over, we both would have sank to the bottom like rocks. But, hey, we were hot and bothered beach bums, and we had to be cool.

Jeeptracks

Although it was a hot, clear, summer day, the bunch of us were getting a little bit soggy. It was approaching sunset, and we had been drinking beers most of the afternoon. We had been cruising the dunes west of Grayton in Hampton's old Willis Jeep, and, as was nearly always the case, we had gotten stuck, big time. Sometimes, when you try to bank off the face of a giant dune on a 45-degree incline, you just lose it, and start to sideslip, wheels spinning out of control, sand spraying, high and mighty. Usually you drift down to a more stable sand surface, and, with a little bit of rocking, you can ease yourself out. This time, that didn't work. The jeep's downward wheels just sank and dug in. The jeep tilted up. Reggie and Wild Bill bailed out quickly, laughing at first, and then cursing as their faces hit the sand and the last of their beers spilled away.

Not being quick enough, I just gritted my teeth and held on as we flipped, all the while listening to Hampton's maniacal laughter followed by the longest continuous creative stream of cursing I have ever heard. Thank God for the roll bar. After the flip, as we came to rest, still tilted sideways at a 45-degree angle, it became apparent that the both of us were still intact, uninjured, and covered in beer-soaked sand. Neither of us had pissed in his pants (I think), which was a small victory, but we were stuck, big time, and we were out of beer.

Being stuck was an inconvenience, and also a serious blow to Hampton's pride. We would have to hoof it back to "town," which was the sleepy little collection of beach cottages called Grayton, and "borrow" someone else's four wheel drive, and hope word didn't get out that we had gotten stuck so bad we needed to be towed out. That was something only tourists did.

That was bad. But being out of beer... that was really bad. It was just minutes to what was promising to be a gorgeous sunset and we were hoping to be able to situate ourselves on the tallest dune, pop open some cold ones, get high, and just drink it in. Now we would have to come up with a plan B.

Hamp knew what to do. "C'mon," he muttered, and we struck out westward, away from Grayton, and towards a singular towering dune. We trudged up the face of it, not knowing what he had in mind. We were headed in the opposite direction from town, a four-wheel drive, and more beer. Does this guy really know what he's doing? We grumbled, sunburned, sandy, tired, and oh so thirsty. When we reached the top, the three of us sat down, and Wild Bill pulled a crumpled baggy out of his shorts. He always came prepared. He proceeded to roll up a big, fat one, which was usually the cure for most ills, and certainly the best way to appreciate a sunset on the beach. But to have nothing to wet our whistles with was a bit of a drag.

Hampton remained standing, and slowly paced around the top of the dune, looking down, as if looking for clues. Finally he found a specific spot, stood and turned facing due north. Then he spread his arms out wide just like an Indian praying to the Sun God, and fell flat on his back in the sand. We all just watched in tired amusement. Hamp had done peculiar things before. This time, he just started digging the sand below his right hand. Shortly thereafter, a triumphant grin appeared on his face, and his hand pulled up a half-full bottle of Jose Cuervo Gold. We all just stared dumbfounded in admiration. The dude had come through again, with style.

He explained later, as we sipped, and toked, and drank in the sunset, that this had been the same dune he had come out to late last weekend, and that this was the exact spot at which he had sort of passed out, and had had enough survival skills left to bury his stash, just before slipping into sandy sleep.

Hampton saved the day, we captured the magnificent sunset in our memories, we got back to Grayton very late that night, and didn't retrieve the Jeep 'til very late in the morning. Just another day at the beach in Seagrove in the seventies.

THE LEGEND OF SHADOW

It's sort of peculiar to think of your dog as "legendary," but I suppose that description might fit our dog, Shadow, real well. She passed away probably in the late part of the eighties, but people talk, and some have photos, of "the dog that water-skied." She really didn't do that; not exactly, but she did several other unique things that made her "almost human" as they say, as if that's a compliment.

She caught fish, for instance. Not only did she sit in the water at the Eastern Lake Inlet, and the lake itself, for hours on end, studying the myriad fishes, minnows mostly, that meandered in front of her paws. Sometimes, after waiting and gazing, and waiting and gazing, she would pounce... and pull up a croaker or something, flapping wildly in her jaws. She would prance up to anyone watching, and usually she would drop it, play with it a bit, and then someone would throw it back. Once in a while, she would swallow one almost whole, but I'm not sure she ever liked fish. My brother, Wilbur, probably spoiled her with the fried egg and cheese he always managed to have "left over" on his plate. Shadow never begged, but always got the leftovers. Shadow never really talked, but she communicated quite well. She would sort of motion towards the door a lot. You could tell when she wished to go to the beach. She would claw at the sliding glass door, or put her nose to it. When you opened it, she wouldn't go out... You shrugged, went back to what you were doing, so important, and then, a little later, she would be quietly looking, again, at the door. You would open it again, she would look, and then she'd give you those puppy-dog brown eyes, and you would get it...She wanted to go to the beach with you! The magic words were "ya want to go to the beach?" and she was the essence of inquisitive play. She roamed the inlet making friends with everybody, all the time. People on the second and third floors of Commodore's Retreat would let her in sometimes like family. Once, a little girl came knocking on my mom's door and asked, quietly, politely, "Can Shadow come out and play?" There was a feeling, that if you mentioned the name "Shadow" almost anywhere in Birmingham, someone would have known this dog.

Besides befriending everyone like the hostess of the inlet, she managed to almost corner a maybe two foot long nurse shark in the shallows...

I said "almost" and "maybe," but she did... She also poked a foot-wide stingray once. I think she learned real quickly, not to do that again. She tried many times to sneak up on one of those sandpipers, but they were quick. I think she played the same game with the herons.

One time, Shadow didn't come home...We always let her roam. She just always came back, and scratched at the sliding glass door. Sometimes, she would roam a full two miles to the Russell's store, and we would find her sitting next to that great old magnolia that use to grow against the store, she would be hyper about getting the squirrels that lived so well in that tree. This one time that Shadow didn't come back lasted three weeks...we were heart-broken...and then, one day she came back, all four paws just torn from running. I mean, how far away is Birmingham, really?

As to the fishing, well, one day, she was sitting in the lake, as she almost always did, and I was working on the shed, as I almost always did, and suddenly she just chomped, and pulled up a croaker that was, at least, one foot long. Casel Morgan happened to be right near, and being the proper fisherman that he was, he cleaned and fried up that fish for us that night, and Shadow, most likely, got the healthy leftovers. This isn't a fish story, this is a dog story.

Sure, you're saying, and the dog water-skied too, huh? Well, no she didn't, technically. She surfed, or rather rode a surfboard behind a boat. I'll admit she had a guy holding the rope (Wilbur would do anything to be in a classic photo), but that was Shadow standing on the nose of that Hansen 50/50 longboard on the Fourth of July sometime in the seventies, and there are dozens of witnesses.

In those days, Seagrove was just a bunch of buddies with a handful of jeeps on the beach, a ski circus on Eastern Lake, and, of course, a dog named Shadow.

GLANCING

I stood, leaned against the bar, a thousand thoughts begging to be left asleep below. So I obliged them with a beer, and then another, just to be sure. The woman across the room totally ignored me, with all her being, and sincerely. She seemed to be the only woman in the room, or perhaps just the best. Of course, she couldn't see me in my blues, chatting with my good friend, Busch. She was tall and tan, with straight, medium length blonde hair, and was wearing a black body shirt under the same old light blue denim work shirt, and it worked on me the same old way. But all of this was extra. She simply had a precious, well-formed face, and her beauty seemed to touch me everywhere she went. A smile, a smirk, a grin, a splash of laughter, and then a pause between breaths, when her mind seemed to be adrift; and it seemed like my thoughts were pressed against the curves of her mouth, like a boy with his face against the pet store window. But still I watched her from across the dimness, and sipped a beer, still my only friend, as I waited foolishly for something called "timing."

But only time slid by. The band filled the room with just the proper rhythmic passion, and I marked my time by tapping on a tinking half gone can of beer, carefully noticing all the changes in the same old people in the same old place, constantly, carefully keeping my awkward eyes on her. It just didn't seem to be fair, the way her eyes played, the way she was such precious friends with everyone.

And I felt so crude and unkept, my hands so restless and stubborn. The words would never come with any assurance. I knew I could possibly interest her, but was it only in my absurdity? Was she ready for a gentle stranger trying to slip out a dark blues? Could she understand that her presence could be catalyst, her smile and words could bring a whole new turn in my path?

The dance of eyes continued: her eyes, my eyes. The glances... And then the surge of imbalance, as I turned the corner of my drunk, and didn't care. It's funny how the loneliness numbs you. You sink so distant that your madness keeps you from a terminal blues. That's the way I stood there, with my present buzz, and my absent heart. My eyes were like cautious eagles flying circles about her hair and face, moods dancing through the music, hoping to catch her eyes with just a whimsical chance...

But the band is winding down and I have spent my change. I grab my coat, but then I hesitate in dramatic departure. She's standing now, so long and tight and slender. She's talking with her back to me. I'm hoping that she'll turn and perhaps I'll catch her. But she doesn't, and my waiting feels too foolish, so I amble towards the door. Wiping dreams away, I glance once more. This time a halfway smile slips from her feelings. At least I know she's noticed. Perhaps we'll meet, perhaps we won't. I pack my thoughts and dreams away; my hands reach for my pockets. It's funny how one smile can fill me up and keep my hopes afloat. I head on home with such an absent-minded grin on my face. I feel just like a schoolboy with his first new crush. And, as I crawl in bed, I am a child once more, wrapped in just the world's love.

Hurricane Opal

The storm brought a change. The storm blew paths to shreds and plans to vapor. The storm turned roads into avalanches and avenues into rivers. Highways were parks for boats and walkways lay dangling in the somber sunlight. Nature had nudged us steadily at 120 mph sustained wind, with a possible storm surge of twenty feet, just a little bit exaggerated. Mother Nature had come in awesome violence and had made herself understood. My reverence was now somehow altered. It wasn't just respect for her force, but more like humility in the inevitability of change. In an instant the bluffs at Seagrove were so much steeper and filled with new clean grandeur. In a fast crashing evening, Eastern Lake pass, wide and proud, was transformed into a gentle stream. The landscape was different. Scattered fragments of homes and docks and walkways littered isolated backwaters and lagoons. Most of the beach was swept flat and disturbingly barren. The only "enduring" landmarks were the buildings, and almost all of them looked a little bit meek, and, even somewhat rattled, that their pride was somehow shaken by the unforgiving storm. Many houses shone their courage and stood grand defiant. But others split apart and were scattered, as surely by chance and whimsy in the wind and the sea's relentless dance, as by any defect in the plans of the people who built them.

Perhaps the most remarkable memories of Hurricane Opal were the three or four days after. The first day was filled with exciting exploration, but after a while you got somewhat numb to the destruction. The lasting memories were of the incredibly calm, peaceful nights that followed the storm. We were without water and food, but that was quickly solved by family and friends who provided me with more pork and beans and cans of Spam than I ever want to see again. I had more ice than I knew what to do with. Although nothing came out of the shower spigots, water for the toilet was plentiful. I just walked over to the lake with my five-gallon bucket, and that minor crisis was solved. When, at last I absolutely had to have a bath, I simply walked into the gulf with my bar of soap.

We were also without electricity, but, you know, that really was something of a blessing. The nights were so clear, the moon so full; it was so calm and peaceful without the glare of streetlights. The beach can be quite awesome when it's bathed in simple moonlight. It was like the good old days of Seagrove. There were no TV's, no stereo, no distractions from the wondrous sounds of the ocean. It was so naturally primitive you could feel God's presence everywhere. No one will believe me, but there was a time when you could walk the dunes and see nothing but more dunes on the horizon. Now you are surrounded with development. You cannot venture anywhere that hasn't been scarred by four-wheelers. Opal brought back the good old days, if only for three or four lovely evenings.

SEASIDE: THE BEGINNINGS

Seaside was probably conceived in the back seat of a Buick. If it wasn't a Buick, it surely was some large American cruising machine rolling down some southern two-lane blacktop with Robert Davis sitting with Daryl in the back seat, perhaps Andre at the wheel. It was here, I think, that the idea for Seaside initially took shape. It was along these highways, somewhere outside of Savannah or Charleston, or cruising south out of Montgomery on highway 331, that Robert saw a vision of the way life was in those gentler years of not so long ago. He saw glimpses of society in the streets and avenues of these sleepy little towns. He saw warmth and friendliness perched beside the picket fences and backyard pergolas. There was something more human in downtowns that rose no more than two or three stories with storefronts of every color and style. It was the colors, shapes, and textures of these gentle places that Robert wished to capture in his little village by the sea. It was with this in mind that he chose the architects that he would employ to design his town.

At least, that is my guess. It would be difficult for me to tell you about all the years of planning that went into Seaside, because I simply wasn't a part of that facet of the endeavor. What I can provide for you is a look into the unfolding of Seaside from the prospective of a native.

My family likes to feel we were some of the pioneers of South Walton County, but in reality we simply found this place a little bit before the rest of the world. In those days it wasn't "South Walton County" or "The Emerald Coast." It was simply Seagrove. It was a pristine stretch of wilderness beach and vast shining sand dunes that wrapped around secluded lakes where you felt God's wonders in the silent glide of a blue heron coming to rest on the mirrored surface of a quiet pond. Seagrove was the heart crush murmur of the surf folding over in perfect rhythm as we strolled along the moonlit sands. Seagrove was all my childhood memories held motionless against the winds of time.

My Father bought an old beach cottage on Eastern Lake in 1959, and from that time forward, we have been calling this place home. My father was an officer in the Air Force and he had truly been all around the world. He could have chosen any place to settle down and think of retirement. He chose Seagrove. It's a possibility he might have flown over this area in an airplane and was captivated by the long stretches of sand dunes punctuated by the coastal lakes. It must have looked like a strand of emeralds strewn across a white velvet cape. Who knows why or when the first inhabitants moved into this area? There were Indians around more than 2,000 years ago, but whether they settled here or just moved through has never been known. But someone at some time named some of the lakes and places of this area many years ago. That someone, perhaps, without too much imagination, named the two largest lakes around, simply, Eastern Lake and Western Lake. Whoever this guy was, it's somewhat obvious where he had to be coming from: Seagrove.

My family found Seagrove via Highway 331, coming south from Selma, Alabama. We came and stayed with friends and fell in love with the place to that familiar old song "Theme from a Summer Place." It was about 1958. It wasn't long before my father discovered the old cottage at Eastern Lake owned by Billy Wesley, one of the descendants of the Wesley family that pioneered Point Washington. It was down way past where the pavement ended on Highway 30-A, which didn't connect through, like it does now. Every village had its own separate winding road in those days that led back up to highway 98, and one barely even knew of the existence of exotic locales like Grayton, Seacrest, or Dune Allen. There was simply Thornton's Grocery in the middle of Seagrove and miles and miles of beautiful wilderness, dotted here and there with an occasional beach cottage. Highway 30-A dead-ended about a half mile west of Seagrove, and maybe a mile and a half east of a small cluster of cider block homes on Montgomery Street. I believe highway 30-A was finished around 1969. Thornton's became Russell's Grocery. The Wheelhouse had its beginnings soon thereafter.

About the only social life around here in the early 70's was hanging around the Old Bulter Store. It was called Grayton Place in those days. A Ping-Pong table, pinball machines, and a jukebox were the major entertainment. Hanging out in the parking lot was where it was happening. What more could you want? We'd grab a cooler full of beer and jump in somebody's jeep and the dunes would be ours. The backside of the store became the Short Branch Saloon for a while, with a pool table and the assorted rascals that use to hang out in places like that.

Hurricane Eloise, in 1975, put an end to the Short Branch, and probably marked the close of an era I like to call the Early Grayton Days. Before long, red clay roads were being built out into the dunes, and this land would never be the same. We all thought it very funny that people, developers, would even attempt to build roads out into the sand. We knew the storms would blow in and just cover them up. But the roads kept coming, and then the asphalt, and then the houses. They came on with their condos and townhouses, and were able to sink a few high-rises, but then the surge of development seemed to subside just a little.

It was in 1981 that people around here first heard of Seaside. There were articles in the papers about a developer that wanted to change Highway 30-A just west of Seagrove so that it took a big northerly course around his land, in order for him to build this new town he designed. Well, the plan to move the highway was just a little too radical and costly, and it went nowhere, and I must admit most of us locals were just a little bit skeptical of just what this guy from Miami had in mind. In my view, I just couldn't see how you could build a new structure and have it hold all the charm and quaintness that old beach cottages always seem to have. I mean, wasn't it all the years of human passage that gave these homes the enchantment that we all felt. I was an early scoffer. Let's just sit back and see what these out-of-towners can do, we said to ourselves.

I was living in Fort Walton during these times, just coming out to do my laundry on weekends at my mama's house. So it was rather easy to stay aloof from Seaside. I just drove by and murmured, hmm, yeah, so they have built one house. Hmm, yeah, so they have built two houses. So what? After all, these were outsiders coming in, and in those days, nobody was really ready for, or was expecting, any change along 30-A. I was a journeyman carpenter in those days, but I felt comfortable not working in Seaside, so I could scrutinize and criticize it freely from a distant perspective. I had already known that Seagrove was something special, and had started buying a piece of land down near the canal, with dreams of someday building a house there, when I paid it off. What was happening in Seaside was a curiosity, but nothing to get overly excited about.

It wasn't until the summer of 1984 that my feelings towards Seaside began to change. There were basically two things that changed my mind. The first thing was that I began to work for Seaside, when the contractor I worked for started building a house in there, and abruptly quit, leaving me the task of finishing it. He didn't want to deal with

these rather unconventional and complicated houses. I felt as if I had been thrown into the breach, as they say, when I was called upon to complete this house, but I loved it. It was the first Rosewalk house, the first three-story house in Seaside, and the first house with a tin roof I had ever worked on. Working at Seaside was an adventure in winging it, because nobody had built houses like this in more than fifty years. There was nobody to ask how to do it, so you just had to figure it out for yourself. Exposed rafters, tin roofs, widow's walks, lattice skirting: this old stuff was something new to virtually all of us. It was challenging and it was fun, just to look around you as you worked, and see all the new and interesting shapes that were growing up all around you.

It didn't happen all at once. The beginning days of Seaside were times of dusty oyster shell roads and a place called the Shrimp Shack for a restaurant. Seaside started from one bare deck overlooking the Gulf. The Plan was never apparent from the beginning, but simply unfolded, gradually, through the months and years. It wasn't just the houses that were different; but the pergolas, the ornate park benches, the winding, landscaped footpaths, the gazebos and the beachside pavilions. When these shapes began to unveil themselves to my eyes, I slowly understood what was evolving all around me.

Perhaps the greatest golden moment happened to me that first summer when I was working on the roof of the second Rosewalk Cottage, the first octagon tower I had ever built. In those days, radios were commonplace on construction sites. It has changed a bit since then. Anyway, I had my radio tuned to a popular station, and really wasn't paying that much attention until I realized that the AC installers, working at the house next door, had their radio tuned to the same station. And all at once there seemed to be a large stereo effect throughout the entire neighborhood, and it was John Lennon singing "...let me take you down, 'cause I'm going to Strawberry Fields, nothing is real, and nothing to get hung about..." And in that shining moment, this place called Seaside had become Pepperland, where everything was wonderful, and music filled the air.

Several months later, I would be sitting in the unfinished first dining room of what is now Bud and Alley's and I had come to watch the very first movie ever shown in Seaside. There were maybe twenty or thirty of us. I really can't remember who was there. It was dark. But the list was something like this: Foley, Stein, Daryl, Robert, Chris, Michele, Tyrone, Warner, Nancy, Kieran, Ernesto, Fred, Alice, Carl, Richard, Jackie, Donna, Steve, Suzette, Potter, Didon, Keith, and a host of others. The movie was "Yellow Submarine." What more can I say?

None of this just happened overnight, but some of it probably happened in the moonlight. Long evenings, tainted with wine and sea breeze, were spent, imagining a town unfolding. Some of it was simply romantic, yet unexpected, such as all the interconnected streets of red brick. In fact, the brick itself, in addition to the gazeboes and pergolas, was one of the first surprises. In the early days, when there wasn't but four or five finished streets in Seaside, they were really only finished in limestone gravel. These were the days when the public works building was just going up, in the back, and Foley's shop was nothing but a Quonset hut tent that Will and Leah had set up back there as the first "architect's camp." Even those of us who worked there at the beginning, were a bit in awe as different parts of the plan came into focus. I suspect the word focus might be a rather peculiar word to associate with that bunch, since sometimes the summer afternoons working at Seaside seemed more like goofy parades of assorted work crews, planners, architects, carpenters, landscapers, and administrators, chatting with purpose, and pointing in such grand gestures. It seemed much more like a circus in the sand. It seemed that something special was surely happening. Every time Seaside unveiled another facet of their plan you couldn't help but admire the vision of it all, and get caught up in the magic.

The other thing that changed my mind about Seaside was the Seaside Grill. It was in this tiny little cafe that the spirit of Seaside was born. It was here where the locals came out to unwind after a hard hot day of banging nails. It was here that the architects drank beer with the carpenters; salespersons had lunch with the landscapers; where the characters that would somehow shape this town, or at least get it going, would congregate. It was here where we first got together to see who we were. We really felt camaraderie in that we were involved in an endeavor that we knew was something very important. We knew it was a departure and it makes all the difference in the world to be working on something that you know will be historically important.

One of the more interesting experiments that Robert came up with in those days was to have the architects work on some of the projects with the carpenter crews. He hoped it would give the architects more appreciation of the fundamentals of building. At the same time, the carpenters might learn more insights into design. In theory, it was a good idea, but in reality, the two cultures probably can't blend too well.

My crew, in those days, consisted of two guys, Richard Davis, an old friend of mine from the "Old Grayton Days" and Robert Strickland, a new found friend from California. Seaside decided to give us an architect named Ernesto as a work partner, but Ernesto never much got into driving nails in the hot sun. He frequently was heard muttering his favorite phrase, "this is notta my job" in his thick Cuban accent, after a few hard hours of work. He did contribute much to the flavor of the conversations with his glowing descriptions of his beloved homeland of Cuba. He would brew us authentic Cuban coffee at our lunch break, which would take some getting used to, but everything was new in Seaside. Although few people are aware of this, Ernesto designed the

Tupelo Pavilion, perhaps the finest and most indelibly defined symbol of Seaside. Some of us will always remember the small, black stray puppy that befriended him, and followed him everywhere, against his wishes. "This is notta my dog" became his new catch phrase. Gary Rodrigue, who was working on the public works building in those days, started calling the dog Ned, which was short for Not Ernesto's Dog.

Jim Foley had the better deal by far. While he was in the middle of adding on the southern porch to the Seaside Grill, he was assigned three architectural students to lend him a hand. Two of them were good-looking young women. It is probably every carpenter's fantasy to be working on the beach with two lovely ladies, everybody just sweating away in the hot summer sun. No doubt, it was a plumb assignment. Foley has always had a reputation for taking a long time on his projects. And this one, no doubt, took as long as possible. Foley ain't no fool.

The late afternoons were spent in furious games of volleyball. One of Foley's students was a small Chinese girl named Ray, and she was just about the most aggressive volleyball player I have ever seen. We would play literally until the sun went down, and then the game usually degenerated into a beer party. We would sit around the edge of the dunes, laughing and joking into the moonrise. One glorious night the beer party segued into skinny-dipping. At least twenty of us just took it all off and made the big plunge. Seaside later became something of a cultural Mecca, but in the beginnings, primitive native rituals ruled the night.

Once in a while, boxing would be the order of the day. Foley trying to get a piece of Willoughby, the major bad-ass from Freeport; or Captain Carl, hobbling gamely pitted against Ray, quick and wiry. Carl was probably more famous for his backwoods wisdom and guitar playing.

I'll never forget his late moonlight rendition of "I've Got It Made On Thirty-A."

Foley actually came very close to finishing the porch that summer. I remember, near its completion, someone bringing in a boombox with nothing but Motown tunes and, we all climbed through the window to christen the new addition to the strains of "I Heard it Through the Grapevine." There was dancing in the streets that night.

We all felt the Grill was our place. It seems like most of us had a hand in some portion of the many renovations and additions that had happened to the place. The Seaside Grill, which is now Bud and Alley's, has had a wonderful history. It started off as two old shacks that were moved in from Panama City by Will and Leah. They were stationed on the edge of the dunes and a deck was built to connect them. About this time, a marketplace was set up on weekends in the parking lot. It was simply picnic tables and umbrellas, but it became the genesis for Perspicasity. Fruits and vegetables were the first commerce in Seaside, perhaps a few t-shirts. The Memorial Day Hobie Cat Regatta spawned t-shirts that are cherished even today for their place in history.

Peter and Susan Mulcahy ran the grill in those days. They boasted the best hamburgers on the Gulf, and it was true. They were great. A hamburger and French fries for $1.95. Beer for fifty cents! No, it wasn't the 1950s. It was the summer of '84.

It wasn't all play. We got some work done, too, in those days. The first couple of Rosewalk Houses grew up. Tupelo Street had perhaps six or seven residents, if you counted Budweiser, Robert and Daryl's dachsund. Savannah Street was forming, and work was started on the Public Works Building down the hill on Forest Street. The much anticipated post office truly put Seaside on the map.

In the back, Foley was setting up shop. Will and Leah had scored a Quonset hut style tent at one of the government auctions and it was set up as the first architect's camp, down in the valley below Forest Street. This is where the architects stayed and played. Anne, Ray, Cary, Ernesto, and Derrick were some of the early settlers in the Seaside Swamp.

The times were fresh with anticipation, and the summers were long golden adventures. As the years moved along, Seaside became more complete and was gently handed over to the shopkeepers and the tourists. The Seaside Grill was transformed into Bud & Alley's. I am personally amazed at how well the brick roads have aged. Perhaps, it's because people who first encounter Seaside almost inevitably get caught up in a honeymoon mode, and seem to float a few inches above the brick. The tight bunch of natives who shaped Seaside in the beginnings, has migrated only slightly. They live, work, and play in Grayton Beach, Pt. Washington and Eastern Lake, but a part of them will always remain in Seaside.

FRAMERS

Although a lot of people might wonder why a person might attempt to make his living, sweating, and straining against heavy lumber and the toils of moving, shaping, cutting, banging, and sometimes bending cantankerous planks and slabs of wood into basically straight, somewhat level, and almost always plumb, structures with roofs that not only dazzle the imagination, but also keep water out, even in a howling, horizontal driving rainstorm, I seem to know or hang out around quite a few nail benders who actually like the lifestyle. The work seems to suit their clothes, there's plenty of sunshine, and no one telling you you can't smoke. You don't necessarily need to be clear-eyed and sharp as a tack every morning, which allows for ample recreational drinking in the off-hours.

Most of them just enjoy the act of building, of creating something out of nothing. The feeling of satisfaction at the end of the day, actually seeing the results of the work you did. It is the art of building, of taking pieces of wood, the bones of dead trees, and somehow stacking them in the proper way, with grace in lines and the satisfaction of a job well done. This, in addition to the camaraderie, is what these guys are out there for. It is to the framer that I truly tip my hat. In the whole process of designing and building, the framer is the craftsman that is overlooked the most. He is the man who has to take these lines and plans and drawings and sketches and devise a way to take just plain common sense mixed with a few good tricks, along with a few good nailers who don't mind the heights, and make a reality: a square, straight, level and plumb house for all the trim carpenters and interior designers in the world to play with. And all the architects of the world to sit back and bask in what they think is their own glory.

Who is the guy that installed the roofline on that house down the street you adore? It was the framer, setting the ridge, running the rafters, decking it in, setting the windows; then, after all that, cutting in a winding staircase going up two and a half floors. It was many days in the hot summer swelter, every now and then catching one of those cool ocean breezes that seem to take your breath away. Many days of cutting, hauling, and nailing pieces of wood together, yet all the work has just a single goal: the culmination of the house, the assembly of all the absolutely astounding array of material that goes into a house, and to do it well. That's what the framer's work is all about. That, and a whole lot of daydreaming.

Yes, daydreaming. One of the best reasons Hampton ever had for being a carpenter, besides the fact the job suited his clothes and his drinking habits, was the time you had for daydreaming. Although there is quite a bit more mental work than people might be aware of, like rafter-cutting and the mysteries of a spiral staircase that are just a few duties that might intimidate the best of brain surgeons, there is also a lot of repetitious work, both nailing and cutting, where it is almost essential to let your mind wander and let your hands and physical skills take over. Carpentry is simply common sense taken to the next degree. Craftsmanship is simply care and patience. A lot of it is manual dexterity and persistence. Your mind can check out for long periods of time while your eyes and your hands put on the finishing touches. That's what art in carpentry really is. I mean, a well-built house or table or cabinet can't help but reflect the time and care put into it. It has literally been caressed and petted in the process of being measured, shaped, sanded, puttied, and finished with layer after layer of caring hands. You can't help but care. The damn thing will probably out-live you. All these structures would survive longer than we will. That's why we try to make them as perfect as we can. To imbue them with the timelessness and perfection we can never obtain.

BEATLES PEOPLE

"...and marmalade skies..." This was perhaps the exact point, in the poetry of the Beatles, where the world changed. Before this time we were simply on a boat, on a river, with tangerine trees. It was still the normal world. And then, with one phrase, we entered something new. Someplace with newspaper taxies...and looking-glass ties...a girl with kaleidoscope eyes... We know from our history, our photos, and our record albums that the Beatles evolved before our very eyes and ears. No musical group changed so much in their career, and in doing so, they changed us, too. We all know that it was a by-product of the psychedelic era, the times of LSD and mind altering drugs. It was a time of freedom. It will be interesting to see how the young people of today will embrace this music. It may not have the taint of "drugs" to them, but might simply be seen as imaginative whimsy. The Beatles started off as a rock n' roll band, but the body of their work is something different, something timeless. Melodic whimsy, cute ditties, interspersed with elegant, haunting images, perfect melodies, and just an incredible ensemble of interesting characters. They truly created a world.

In all the punditry and profundity surrounding the Beatles, I find it very strange that little mention was ever made of their storytelling abilities. Although a majority of their greatness became evident in their simple, short, songs filled with unique beautiful melodies, beneath the surface of many of their songs was a personal story written about people we felt like we knew. Have you ever thought about all the named characters that populated the world of Beatles songs?

Of course, the famous ones pop into mind first. We all know who Sgt. Pepper is, and who cannot have beautifully haunting visions of Lucy in the Sky with Diamonds? Billy Shears was the gentleman that introduced us to the celebrated Mr. Kite and his partners, the Hendersons. A splendid time was guaranteed for all. Lovely Rita, meter maid, was, of course, the girl that got away.

But, this was hardly the only album that was filled with Beatles-people. Eleanor Rigby was a perfect portrait of someone's sad, lonely aunt, and Father McKenzie will always be darning his socks when there's nobody there. Somewhere out there Lady Madonna is trying to make ends meet.

There were some very early people we didn't know much about: Mr. Moonlight, Anna, Michelle; the Beatles were young and in love and everything and everyone was rather simple. Then there were others we were introduced to on the White Album that filled a world with so much more depth, variety, and satire. There was always the beautiful Julia, but now there was Sexy Sadie, Dear Prudence, Honey Pie, and, of course, the silly Desmond and Molly Jones. What sort of imagination can produce a fellow like Bungalow Bill living next door to the Mother Superior?

Of course, some of the most memorable people stood out in their short story of Rocky Raccoon. A whole story wrapped around an ensemble of characters. There was Doc, Danny Boy, and the gal "whose name was McGill, but she called herself Lil, and everyone knew her as Nancy." In one line, this woman had not one, but two mysterious pasts. It was like an entire opera in a three-minute song.

When you talk about mystery, who in the world was Semolina Pilchard, climbing up the Eiffel Tower? The Walrus? The Eggman? All just characters weaving through a tapestry of astonishing sounds and musical imagery.

Near the end of their musical journey, the Beatles brought even more of their characters into our lives. "Here come ol' Flat-top, he come grooving up slowly." We get a short glimpse into the lives of Mean Mister Mustard and Polythene Pam, as well as a beautiful vision of the Sun King.

I'm sure there are Beatle-people I have forgotten through the years. I'm reminded of Sweet Loretta Modern, and JoJo, who was trying to get back. And Jude, who was reminded that "the movement you need is on your shoulders." I'll always be able "to put an old LP on the turntable" and revisit these people that the Beatles brought into our lives through sheer imagination, and I'll always be able to rekindle that hope that all you need is love.

THE STUFF THAT SHIRTS ARE MADE OF

I feel a need to talk about clothing, specifically the rather unfair exaltation of blue jeans. Sure they are functional, sturdy, casual wear, that we all feel comfortable and stylish in. They can be sexy as well. My major complaint is they become even more revered as they become faded, tattered, and even torn in the knees. "Shabby chic" is what you could call them, I guess. They have become something of a sex symbol when they are reduced to cut-offs and surround the shapely bottoms of young, slightly less than innocent, females. While I have truly admired a great pair of faded, provocatively torn blue jeans time and time again, I feel they have unjustly overshadowed many a fine shirt.

Let me explain, if I can. As a construction worker, I have gone through many, many pairs of Levi's, blue jeans, dungarees (does anyone really call them dungarees?) whatever. But I have been through even more shirts, and it is a sad, sad tale.

As I began to enter my forties, I stopped wearing t-shirts to work. I thought maybe I had matured to the point where they might make me seem too young and I would not retain the respect I thought I deserved. Not really...I just thought I looked better in regular, buttoned shirts and it ensured that I would have a pocket to keep my reading glasses close by. I began to buy cotton work shirts, but they were rather boring monotones and I felt cooped-up. The alternative was wearing "older" shirts and this is how it all goes down.

First a shirt is bought because it catches my eye and seems stylish and cool. It hangs in my closet for months, and, only occasionally, I will wear it when I go out on the town. After a while, the shirt slips out of favor or out of style, but it remains a good old stand-by. I might wear it to the store or something, but new shirts have usurped its position as a possible "date" shirt. It remains wrinkled, but o.k. I can always wear it around the house.

After a while, it starts to look even less stylish and has lost virtually all its cool. Then it is quietly condemned into use as a work shirt. A work shirt takes a beating. It endures constant punishment: the baking sun, the dirt, the sawdust, and, most of all, the constant sweat.

The work shirt gets deposited on the floor very quickly at the end of the day. Gone are the days when it is hung back up nicely or put on a peg to be worn a second proud time. No, the work shirt is tossed in the bin, and washed with indifference and even callousness. A work shirt is never ironed. Slowly, worn spots appear, perhaps a button is lost, and then there is the fraying, oh the cruelty of the fraying. You might wear a frayed work shirt maybe once or twice, but then a rip will appear.

At that point comes the ultimate insult. The shirt becomes a "paint shirt." How sad and cruel it is when that once proud shirt, that you may have once worn to boogie down at the local disco, realizes that you care so little that you risk it taking on splatters of paint with indifference. The shirt can sense your embarrassment to ever wear it in public again and surely knows its days are numbered.

The slide continues fast from there. Soon the shirt gets too gunked up to wear and it becomes a rag. First a "clean rag", used to clean brushes, perhaps. Sometimes the rag is washed or rinsed out again, but it is no longer a shirt, no longer will it see the sunlight, feel the salty sweat, or dream of the disco lights. It is used and used again, sometimes on the sink, sometimes on the floor. Each time, it soaks in just a little more dirt.

Then, one fateful day, the once proud and stylish shirt must meet its final destiny. It may come at the end of the brutal, yearly cleaning of the tub scum, or at the sudden unexpected disposal of the puppy's "mistake." It is usually quick and merciful, the top of the trash can flips up, the shirt-rag is tossed, and the garbage truck comes tomorrow and takes it away to its final resting place, the dump.

Blue jeans never seem to suffer this fate. Blue jeans with tattered knees and worn-out butts just seem to age so well. We keep them, even the old 32's, hoping to one day shed those middle-age pounds, and reunite with ancient bohemian days, flipping Frisbees in the park.

Shirts just seem to fall by the wayside, sad yet colorful. But, I'll always remember you, my fair, fashionable friends, may you sway sweetly on that great clothesline in the sky.

RARE MORNING

The woman, lying beside me, rolled over in the early morning, and put her arms around me. She whispered in my ear: "Wake up sleepyhead. You have to take me canoeing." It was five o'clock in the morning, but the sun was already starting to bring a soft haze of light into our bedroom. I climbed out of bed and got the coffee started. I walked to the window beside the Christmas tree. Although it was almost the middle of December, the weather was darn near perfect. There was ever so slightly a chill in the air, which I love. And the lake was absolutely mirror smooth. There are rare days and then there are really rare days. There have been days, in my past, when the lake was so magically gorgeous, but I was so absolutely alone, and a solitary canoe trip was just a confirmation of loneliness. But this morning was a very rare day, when I was absolutely in love with this wonderful woman, who could read my feelings so well. It was her idea to get out on the lake for our morning coffee, and it was a perfect day to do so. We walked down to the lake, our flip-flops slapping happily on the dock. We eased the canoe in so gently we never spilled a drop of our coffee. We were expert aficionados of the dawn. I brought my camera, and we just drifted and swirled on the mirror of the lake, and time just stood still for us. We captured the moment, before the sun's soft arrival, and simply shared the moment with the seabirds. It was a truly rare, wonderful morning, and I have never been so in love.

THE BUTTERFLY

Drawing in a deep breath, Hampton lifted the framed wall into the air and stood it. It was just another wall on just another house. It was repetitious but essential. It had lost much of the magic of accomplishment but still contained the honest satisfaction of construction, that intangible feeling that kept him at his job, however grueling it might sometimes be. In other ways, it was truly more enjoyable than any conceivable office or indoor job.

As Hampton lifted the frame, a solitary butterfly gently flew through it, breezing through that imaginary wall that existed only in Hampton's mind. It was simply a butterfly. But Hampton quietly contemplated how many years (decades, more like centuries, perhaps millenniums) would pass before a butterfly would fly though that space again. That space would soon become layers of insulation, siding, sheetrock, paint, perhaps a picture, and then someday that wall would fall. It would fall someday. And then, perhaps, a butterfly would traverse that plane again.

Hampton simply drank of the sweet singularity of the moment and then went about the day, with a somewhat curious sense of serenity. It was just one of those strange, quirky sort of thoughts that popped into his mind sometimes. Interesting, entertaining, somewhat intriguing, and yet, so totally useless. A bit like a postcard. He pondered the intricacies, and eccentricities of his thoughts, always hoping that they would lead him to somewhere.

Hurricane Flotsam

After the hurricanes of 2005, it was hard to find a silver lining. The battering we took from Ivan and Dennis made the memories of Opal seem like a dress rehearsal. The bluffs of Seagrove that stood so tall and majestic, for most all of my life, were now chopped in half and had been eaten by the ocean. The erosion that Hurricane Ivan and then Hurricane Dennis had wrought had transformed this wondrous stretch of pristine dunes into a war zone. Helpless humans were now scrambling to save their houses from the might of Mother Nature's wrath. It was so ugly and puny: the way they moved in with dump trucks and bulldozers to re-shape what God had given us. This was really the true profanity: the way we had to preserve our "wealth" with arrogant misuse of diesel power and the ability to build endless ugly seawalls to attempt to keep the ocean away from our doors. "What have they done to the Earth?" Jim Morrison asked, way back in '68, "What have they done to our fair sister? Ravished and plundered and ripped her and bit her, stuck her with knives in the side of the dawn, tied her with fences and dragged her down..."

I guess I've become a little bitter watching the change in my hometown of Seagrove. It seems like I've spent this whole year doing nothing but cleaning up debris after hurricanes. This, however, can be a very revealing exercise. You move your way very slowly through the tangled mess, and different pieces and parts of human life emerge. Probably the single most salient parts of the debris are the tangled masses of sea oats and weeds that twist and tie around everything. Interspersed in these are pieces of driftwood and loose lumber. The shear amount of 4x4's and 2x6's is what is truly amazing. Every dune walkover in the vicinity seems to be piled on my lake shore. And at first it seems exciting. All that lumber: mine, all mine. And then you have to think, how am I going to untangle it? How am I going to sort through the rubble and pick out the good pieces? How am I going to unbolt and un-nail these partial constructions? There are so many dock sections completely intact and useable but they are simply too heavy and always in the wrong place to get at them. They are all so diverse: they never fit back together again. It, almost inevitably, becomes a matter of dismantling them, pulling the nails out, then stacking the pieces until you can come up with some idea or project to use them again.

After weeks of procrastination and some clean up, you resolve to burn most of it. Then you find out how hard it truly is to rake the sea oats and weeds that are so solidly clumped together. It's all hand-to-hand fighting to get the flotsam and jetsam into the flame. Then you come to the most insidious trash of them all: the plastic. The most predominant articles in all the debris that washes up on your beach, from who knows where, is the plastic. Plastic buckets, plastic shovels, plastic duckies, boats, and froggies aren't so bad, but there are also thousands of much smaller pieces of wrappers and bottle caps and disposable lighters. A dozen cricket lighters washed up on my lakeshore. And bottle caps. You cannot rake these menacing little pieces up without taking up all your topsoil and vegetation. You cannot ignore them and hope they fade into the landscape because they are all so colorful. Bright blue and white and red little plastic bits and pieces of litter. Bottle caps, Styrofoam cups in scattered pieces everywhere. It's eerie to think of our vast oceans are covered in a film of all this litter.

Even after the major work is done, like rebuilding the dock on the lake for the third time, there seems to always be more little bits of flotsam and jetsam to pick up... and this is where I found the silver lining...the treasure. In all the pieces of lumber and pieces of docks and walkways, there was just a vast tangle of seaweed and sea oats. After all the big stuff had been removed, after all the brown and gray organic stuff had been dragged away, there was left an array of tiny bits of color. As you walked the ground, these tiny bits of blue and red and yellow jumped out at you. You reach down to investigate and often all you come up with is a bottle cap or a Bic lighter; a baby's sand shovel, or a golf ball. But every now and then, I found a treasure. In the mud and weeds, tucked away, half buried in the sand, I found an armyman. To you, it might seem like a tiny rubber/plastic toy replica of a U.S. soldier that you have seen so many times before; but to me, it was one of my lost soldiers, one of my men that I had misplaced so many years ago. And now the fate of the winds and the waves had brought him home to me.

Each time I found another armyman, it was like finding a long lost friend, a shining piece of my childhood that had fallen away from my grasp and had somehow been lost in the tides of time. How can we become so cool, so grown-up, and so mature that we let these little treasures drop from our hands? Can anyone really tell me with unwavering certainty that any of these five little soldiers were not one of mine? I mean, if one thing is clear through these relentless storms, it is that plastic endures forever. Wood pieces scatter and break apart, their metal nails and screws rust away. Brick and stone get buried in the sand, and sink, perhaps, to a different century, but plastic just bobs on the surface; bright, colorful, cheap, and utterly worthless.

Except for my armymen... These little men take me back, directly to my childhood, to those early days of huge grand Christmas after Christmas, and endless days playing army in the sands of Seagrove.

MELODIES IN THE MAKING

"It was twenty years ago today, Sgt. Pepper taught the band to play..." It occurred to me one day that Seaside is the Beatles. In terms of planned communities, Seaside is simply a phenomenon. It has reached a status in planning and architecture that is singular and lasting. What the Beatles did in the realm of music, Seaside has surely matched in urban planning and architecture. Just as a myriad of musicians and bands have acknowledged that the Beatles were the major influence in their careers, and indeed, their lives, one would be hard-pressed to find any contemporary planned development that did not owe much of its inspiration to Seaside.

I make this comparison to try to see the developments in South Walton, and indeed, the rest of the country, in the proper light. There is very little use in comparing Rosemary Beach, or WaterColor, or Alys Beach, in contrast to Seaside, but rather we should view these contemporary "musicians" as their own unique acts. Surely growing up in the 70's surrounded by the Beatles influence, people like Sting, or the band U2, had to have forged a reverence for the Beatles, just as they attempted to shape a whole new sound. Likewise, villages like Carillon, Caribe, Frangista and others, have, perhaps, performed "covers" of the "songs" Seaside has written, on their way to composing their own tunes. Variations on a theme have inevitably occurred. Seaside's pastel love songs have been changed into an earthy jazz in Rosemary, perhaps the artists of WaterColor and WaterSound have formed a fusion of blues and classic rock. Think Caribe, and you're thinkin' reggae, mon. Seaside didn't invent gazebos, picket fences, and pergolas: the melodies that pervade each brick-lined avenue, each "album," if you will. Likewise, the Beatles didn't invent rock and roll. They both borrowed the proper proportions of the past, borrowed a few riffs here and there, and tempered it with their own style and vision, to create a lasting legacy from which we all can build, and sing along. The most wonderful part of both music and architecture is that once it's created, no one can own it. It's out there forever in the fabric of our lives. To venture down the streets of Seaside to the center of

Ruskin Place can be as visually enthralling to the eyes as a passage of Mozart is to the ears. They are both such uplifting experiences. At the same time, a stroll past the shops surrounding Central Square can be as whimsical as Jimmy Buffet. It's all simply music to the eyes. To paraphrase the Beatles (apologies to Paul): "And in the end, the beauty we enjoy is equal to the beauty we construct." Or something like that.

ROCK AND ROLL

I'm not sure people really understand where rock and roll comes from. I know that it is a music that has been written about like no other music in existence. Jazz has always been appreciated but never much written about. Jazz is just so cool and anonymous. Classical has been written about but mostly in the halls of academia. Rock n' roll has been written about by nearly everybody but no one really has a good answer as to where it comes from. I know I am being most presumptuous in thinking I might know, but I do believe I have a clue.

Having been a carpenter, working, with someone building a house right next to you, I have had an unusual insight. You're busy, absorbed in building whatever it is you're working on. You're measuring, sawing, banging, driving nail after nail. Bang, bang, bang, the rhythm of your hammer on your woodwork. Then, every once in a while, you go bang, bang, bang, in that natural rhythm that it takes to drive a nail, and you hear another bang, bang, bang, and, at first, it sounds like an echo... but no, it couldn't be. And then you think someone is answering you, mimicking you... but no, that isn't it. The other guy, the carpenter next door, he's simply hitting his nail in the same basic rhythm as you. It's really just a fundamental rhythm that your body automatically knows that will drive that nail or anything else you need to hit upon.

There is rhythm that is so very fundamental it was probably used in some of the very first instances that man used his hands to pick up something and pound upon something else. The rhythm comes from the human body itself. The beat has always been there. We simply reconnect to a rhythm that has been inside us from the beginning.

FOOLISH

DEAR LOVED ONE,

Any foolish man, who is foolishly trying to "win the affections" (please picture this phrase with GIGANTIC quotation marks) of the object of his admiration (you), would be foolishly remiss, if he did not try to fool said admiree (I'm not sure that's really a word) into thinking he was actually creative, by foolishly submitting some of his ancient, adolescent poetry for her inspection/rejection. This action cannot be seriously considered "romantic" any more than giving said admiree a magnolia blossom that "fell" into his pocket. All rights to be foolish (and still be friends) are hereby forever reserved.

With tongue and foot,
In cheek and mouth,
Respectively,

Hampton Echoes

HUMOR

A strange thing happen to me lately...I found my sense of humor again. I'm not sure where it was. Perhaps it was buried under the pile of divorce papers I had stowed away in the basement. Perhaps it had run off with my money on a joyride to Mardi Gras. I hadn't seen my sense of humor in a long time, but there it appeared one day, grinning from ear to ear, giggling and carrying on with that silly girl at Seaside. Hanging out with her was to my sense of humor as pushups were to my exercise regime. Being around her makes me laugh so much, but it made me silly and clever just to keep up. It was as if she had strengthened my sense of humor. And I have to love her for that, or maybe just tease her some more.

A Bridge Too Far

Richard was beginning to slur his words. This wasn't a very good omen, since he was the one in charge of rigging the dynamite. It could have been the beers, or that last shot of tequila. I was beginning to think the whole operation was in jeopardy. Of course, the whole plan began out of a strange sense of foolishness and futility. I'm not sure how it grew from a silly hope-filled pipedream into a soaking wet reality. But here we were, soaking wet, because we were out in a small johnboat in the middle of Choctawhatchee Bay on a moonless night and the wind had kicked up to about 12 knots. The time was 12:40 a.m. and we were within about 30 yards of the 331 Bridge. It was early April, so the brackish spray from the bay wasn't too terribly cold. I was more worried about the dynamite. In fact, I was worried about the whole damn plan.

It seemed so simple a few months ago. We were all hanging around the Short Branch Saloon in Grayton Beach, on a cold, wet winter's night, shooting pool, drinking beer, the usual. We never had long winters in northwest Florida, but, on the few really cold days we had, we seemed to have a dampness that made it an all the more bitter, biting cold. This was one of those nights.

We were all content to just drink our beer and get toasty. Sometime around ten o'clock a guy came into the bar, obviously a tourist.

"Hey guys, I got stuck in the sand, can you help me out?" he said. There was a deafening silence. Richard shot the six ball in the corner by a double bank. He just grinned as I shook my head. The guy piped up again. "I sure could use some help..." he pleaded so earnestly.

"I dunno..." was about all that came out of me.

"I'll buy you guys a case of beer," he said. The words came out fast and hit their mark.

"You got a deal, dude," I said, as Wild Bill just kind of grumbled. "Where's your car?"

"Just down the beach," he said.

Well, "just down the beach" is a relative term, so when we ventured out into the bitter cold, we had no idea what we were getting into. We all headed out with this guy from Ohio, tromping through the deep thick sand on a damp, cold December night and we thought we were going a hundred yards or so. Most idiots that try to drive a standard car on the beach do not get very far. Somehow this guy had gotten over half a mile west of Grayton and had bogged down in soft sand up to his axle. Now, a lot of times when somebody gets stuck, all you really have to do is tell them to straighten their front wheels, so they are not plowing through the sand, rock the car once or twice, forward and back, and then just ease the car out, giving it just a little bit of gas. You have to ease it out, not gun it. Then you take their twenty or forty bucks and whisper "see ya."

This was not one of those times. This was a case where the three of us had to dig out a good long trench in the front and back of both rear tires with our hands, and put whatever driftwood we could find under the tires to get a little traction. This was one of those times when the three of us had to strain our nuts off to push this fool's car, as the sand was spraying everywhere and we were yelling at the top of our lungs: "Easy, dammit, easy. Don't gun it!"

With a monumental effort, we got him going, only to have him bog down once more and we had to go through the whole process once more. The things a man would do for a case of beer... This time we got Richard in the driver's seat because it was a long, perilous haul to get any car up from the somewhat packed sand at the beach, through the deep sand up to Grayton proper. All we could think about was the warmth of the Short Branch and that cold beer waiting for us.

Richard came through like a champ. Once he got going, he knew just how to keep it going, with just the minimum, easy touch of gas to carry through. The rest of us trudged on, through the fog, to the bar. We were waiting, cold and damp, when Richard walked in. "Where's the dude?" he said to us, as we wondered the same thing.

"I thought he was with you," was the same reply. Richard realized he should not have left the keys in the car. We simultaneously heard the rumble as the tourist from hell cranked up his car and sped off without even a thank you, much less the case of beer. It was a learning experience that put us over the top.

From that cold day in December until now, we had planned out the attack. Our goal was rather simple, if not downright primitive: Restore this island to its natural setting. If you think about it, South Walton is an island. There are just three bridges that bring in all the tourists, all the outsiders. We can preserve this wondrous, beautiful, pristine stretch of sand dunes and scrub oaks. All it would take is the demolition of three small bridges.

The plan was simple, sort of. Wild Bill would do the deed from the north. He would be coming down from Freeport, barreling in with his horse trailer in tow, and then just swerve into a jack-knife. The trailer would be empty and just a bunch of hay would be strewn all over the highway. But the effect would be perfect: the roadway would be blocked for hours.

The south side would be handled, a bit differently, by Gideon. After hearing from Bill that the north side was blocked, he would wait until all cars had passed, somehow stopping the northbound cars, but letting the southbound stragglers slip on by. I never was quite sure was his plan was, but I believe it had something to do with his twin sister's hooters.

The fact is, all plans of mice and men go awry, so they say. And yes, this one bit the dust. Not only did Bill not manage to roll his rig, but Gideon couldn't quite get his sister to leave the bar, with her booty, in time to make the mark. And, as for the A-team, aiming gamely for the center of the bridge, with our sticks of soggy dynamite, we simply had more shots of tequila than would have been prudent for a scheme of this stature. Plus, we couldn't stop giggling. We knew we would blow it, and perhaps blow ourselves up in the process, so we aborted back to the Short Branch Saloon.

Yes, it's true, because of our incompetence, and the other two bridges, all tourists coming to South Walton after the mid-seventies, are all our fault. But, hey, we did give it a shot.

FURTHER

What I'm wanting to say is this...I want to be complete, I want to use every part of me in the best way, and though, I love, I truly love, being friends with you, I want to be all I can be and do all I can do, as a man, to touch you, and caress you. I have an intellect, yes, I have words that bring my mind across to you, but, I have arms, and hands, and lips... There is no meaning in my arms, if I can't wrap them around you, profound in my adoration of the curves of your body. There is no purpose in my hands, if they cannot search your skin, every shape and temperament. There's no essence in my lips, if I can't taste your neck, your eyes, your smile, as your mouth meets mine. There's no soul being used and needed in me without the curiosity of you wishing to meet me further.

Nantahala

One solitary leaf floated gently from the skies above. I watched it slowly drift down, swaying from side to side. I watched it as our raft-full of adventurers floated down the river in the midday sun. The leaf came from one of the hundreds of thousands of colorful trees that carpeted the towering mountains that framed the gorge we traveled through. The leaf's journey intersected our journey in a bright shimmering moment, and then settled on the bubbling waters for a quiet, endless trip somewhere far downstream. I hoped to catch the leaf in my hand but instead my hand came to rest in the hand of my lover, my friend, the woman I'm making The Journey with. Nature's beauty completely surrounded us, with blue sky, sunshine, bright orange hillsides, and the rushing river, crashing all around us in brisk, cold, crashing, challenges.

Just the day before, we had gone searching for the waterfalls, and had found them, one by one. We had kissed beneath the wildest one, just as the sun emerged from the morning mist and the trees glistened in a dazzling gold-lined rainbow. The road trip that afternoon was like a gliding afterglow, winding around every rocky turn in awe of the spectacle of crashing waters and timeworn rocks. We were tired and happy campers as we drove on into the Squire's Inn, and we slept well, as we awaited the next morning's adventure.

Early the next morning, shortly after a wonderful breakfast, we hustled down to the depot and caught the train up the mountain to where the raft trip departed. We rumbled up the tracks and went back in time as we saw old schoolhouses and weather-beaten barns slide by. We clattered past hundred-year-old trestle bridges and caught glimpses of waterfalls and scary caves. The conductor filled our ears with tales of the Indians who first settled the Nantahala River Gorge, the land of the midday sun.

After the raft trip, we ventured on to the Chalet Inn, a truly magical little valley bed and breakfast that gave us just a luscious taste of Europe deep in the heart of the North Carolina foothills. We went exploring up and around their nature paths, climbing to the ridges and winding through the valleys. Every now and then we would venture onto a bench or hammock for a much needed respite. Then we would venture on and simply drink in the marvelous countryside. Near sunset, we rested on a park bench overlooking a valley, and we kissed passionately, renewing our love once more in this wonderful, golden setting.

We arrived back at the Chalet near dark and slept soundly under down-filled comforters as the moonlight trickled in along with the sounds of a mountain brook. We awoke the next morning to the best of breakfasts: homemade breads and sweet rolls, blueberries, poached eggs, and hot, Dutch coffee. Our hosts were so charming, we felt pampered and perfectly tranquil at this wonderful little getaway in a valley way off the beaten track.

Even though we had to travel on, our hearts will always remember our favorite little spot.

TEARS

On the morning of December 11, 1980, I watched the news on television. I read the news that John Lennon was dead and I felt like I had to cry. This man was my friend. He sang and lived ten thousand miles away for most of my life, yet I loved him, I felt I knew him. He was my friend.

I had to go to work. I rolled a joint. I drove out early in my pick-up, and cruised solemnly to the Gulf, glaring east into the soft, cool morning. I pushed in a Beatles tape and took a couple of tokes. I felt I had to cry. I couldn't. I worked a long, full day and came home, more dreary than tired. I took a quick shower, and sat down to watch the CBS news, with just a towel around me. Walter Cronkite devoted nearly twenty minutes on stories about John and the Beatles. They showed the first story they ever did on them, November 21, 1963. They played "A Day in the Life" and showed the people standing around John's last home, crying in the streets.

And I cried, as good, soft, salty, unrestrained tears fell down my face as I sat naked, dripping wet, like a baby. And I cried until I knew what tears were for...

All the tears that fall, those totally emotional, painful, joyful, expressions that turn biological in the human body, what is their purpose? All those screaming tears of joy at Beatles shows, all those tears falling in New York, London, here...All the tears of lovers in ecstatic embrace, all the tears of the mother at birth, and the tears of her child, all the tears of laughter, the tears of pain, death, and mourning, and the tears of childish glee...

They all flow down in strange and endless windings, they merge with the fabric, they soak through the soil, they ride gravity inevitably to their home in the ocean. Our tears return our salt to the sea where we will once again nourish new life, perhaps, retrieving the balance of nature we have so vainly tripped.

The Old Cabin

After my divorce, I retreated back to a little beach cabin that I considered my cave, my fortress of solitude. It was a small place, about 20 feet by 30 feet, and the kindest way to describe it would be to call it primitive. If I were to be a romantic, I could call it a beach shack. It was covered on the outside with vinyl siding that hid the rustic pine siding beneath. I had seen this old house for decades, so I knew what it looked like underneath. I once did some carpentry work on it years ago when a car spun off the dirt road and rammed into the side of it. The main reason it was covered in vinyl was to cover that boo-boo and the years of neglect that was obvious on the old siding. It was very basic construction. No plywood sheathing, no tar paper moisture barrier, just 2X4 studs, with the siding on the outside and old fiberboard paneling on the inside. There was no insulation. In the summertime, as long as I had the window air conditioner cranked up, this wasn't much of a problem. However, when that first winter came, I knew something had to be done. I can remember one warm autumn night when I went to sleep with just a sheet over me, and being startled awake as a cold front easily penetrated the floors and walls of my bleak little house, and I was forced to rummage through all my junk in search of a blanket. Since I was aware of all the gaping holes in the siding beneath the vinyl, and the utter lack of anything but air inside the walls, it dawned on me that about an eighth inch of vinyl was all that was going to be standing between my naked body and any and all arctic blasts that winter. Something would have to be done.

Don't get me wrong. I mean, I did have a small space heater and I did have electricity, just not much of it. The circuit breakers in this shack were just four of the old screw-in glass type that weren't all that easy to find replacements for. The wiring was scary, to say the least. I could lay on the couch with my blanket and watch TV, somewhat comfortably, as long as my little 1800 watt space heater was not too far away. But, if I got hungry, and tried to pop some dinner into the microwave, the fuse would blow. Although there was a total of four fuses, it seems virtually everything, except one light bulb in the back bedroom, was tied to just one fuse. Then I would be searching for a flashlight, to go searching for a spare fuse, to replace the blown fuse, in the cold and dark. Something would have to be done.

One of the first things I did was get new wiring. I didn't do it myself, but got a couple electricians who put in just about everything. One thing I did do was put some insulation in the walls. One of the most perplexing things about the cabin was the ceiling. The original ceiling was old dirty stained Celotex tiles, kind of like cardboard. The previous owner, rather than deal with replacing them, just installed a dropped acoustic ceiling, which never was really attractive, and made it impossible to replace the paneling. To install some new insulation I loosened some of the paneling just enough to cram fiberglass insulation up as far as I could. Primitive, but effective.

The most important thing I did was install a wood-burning stove. My landlord had bought one, years ago, and had it sitting in his garage for a long time, never getting around to installing it. I managed to piece together a bunch of old Mexican tile and made a hearth. I painted the old fake brick behind it a compatible color and installed this great old wood-burner. It was amazingly effective in heating that little house. It was in December when I got it operational, and my electricity bill for January was $24! I would make a ritual of bringing in fire wood during the middle of the day and have it ready for the cold winter nights. I would fill the firebox when I went to bed, and in the mornings there would be just enough glowing embers to stoke a new comforting fire.

I loved this little beach shack. Although I left it when Hurricane Opal turned into a Category 4 and came bearing down on me, I knew I would come back soon. I hit the road, headed towards Tallahassee, and, in my mind, I was waving goodbye to my sweet little house, with my brand new Hewlett Packard 396 sitting inside it. I left, and retreated to Tallahassee, to stay with my brother. The power went out even in Tallahassee, and we watched the news on a four-inch battery-powered TV. We saw Dan Rather, doing his news report, while clinging to a palm tree, in fifty mile per hour winds, in Panama City.

But, believe it or not, by 2 o'clock the next morning, I was headed back to my shack, whether Opal was over or not. On the television radar, in Tallahassee, it looked to me, as if the storm had passed into Alabama, and I was so concerned about getting back, that I just headed out west on I-10. It really didn't seem too bad, but it was a little bit disconcerting that I was one of the only cars heading west and there was an avalanche of headlights heading east. It felt like sixty mile an hour winds, but it was steady from the south. While on the interstate I felt safe, but when I turned south on highway 79, near the town of Vernon, it was a different matter. I was driving mostly straight into the wind on a two-lane blacktop, and I would have to drive around an occasional tree that had fallen and blocked the road. I was getting a bit concerned, but there was no turning back at this point. I really don't remember being scared, but more a feeling of being intensely alive and alert.

I had beer on board, but had the presence of mind not to partake. I had a plan. I would take highway 20 west towards Freeport, try to turn south down the 331 causeway, and if the bridge was impassable, I could always crash at my girlfriend's place in Freeport.

I never made it to Freeport. The howling winds didn't stop me, but a huge pine tree had fallen over the road, with no possibility of driving around it. I took this opportunity to relieve myself on the side of the road, and yes, even though I surely did not piss into the wind, it was a messy adventure. The wind still seemed like 60 mph.

I head back down 79, even though the radio had said all roads into Panama City Beach were closed. And sure enough, just as soon as I came upon the intersection of 79 and Back Beach Road, the street lights were flaying wildly in the gale force winds, and soon there was a policeman knocking on my window. He gave me two choices: he could arrest me on the spot, or I could voluntarily follow him to the station house, until the storm was over. I took the latter.

They took my keys at the station house, and told me to take a seat in the lobby. There were no lights. Apparently, all the power, all along Panama City Beach, was out, and I could see the dispatcher handling phone calls using flashlights. There were a couple other strangers in the dim light of the lobby, and I assumed they were rapists or murderers. After a good little while, I struck up a conversation with them and found out they were a married couple, who owned a limousine service out of Dothan and that they were there because they had driven Dan Rather down there, earlier in the afternoon.

And, as oddly as it seems, it wasn't more than an hour later that the inner door to the station house opened, and who else, but Dan Rather, and his entourage, emerged into the darkened lobby, talked for a few minutes, then left on some errand out into the wildness of the storm. I decided not to try to shake his hand, and introduce myself as the dumb-ass that tried to drive through a hurricane.

About dawn, when the winds had died to below 40mph, they let me leave the station house, and I limped on home to my shack. I was weary, and my eyes were filled with scenes of awesome destruction, but my home was, for the most part, intact. My sweet, cherished little cabin, had survived another major storm, as it had done so many times in the past. I actually kissed my 1990 Chevy Silverado for bringing me through one of the wildest trips of my life.

The Second Sand Bar

I probably haven't told you about Hamp fishing from a scaffold set up on the second bar. I haven't told you, because I didn't really see it, but I believe it. Someone told me the story, and he or I may have been drunk at the time, which really doesn't matter much, because it sounded so satisfyingly real, that I have no doubt that it happened.

This is the way it probably went down. Hamp got a couple of the guys together, down near Grayton. It was, probably, Richard's johnboat, and some scaffolding, most likely, borrowed discreetly, from a Warnerworks jobsite. I haven't got a clue what year or what month it was, but the cobia were running. Now, the standard way of finding cobia is by fishing from some big old boat with a tower, so you can perch and watch and find them slipping thru the surf. It you don't have a boat built for that, you are shit out of luck.

These guys, however, were not in possession of a fishing boat. They were in possession of a little bit of inspiration. The only thing about spotting cobia is getting high...and the easiest way to get high is to build yourself a platform. The simplest way to build a platform is to use scaffolding. Two frameworks of iron, two cross braces, and you have it.

They must have had a bunch of beer. It's easy to have inspiration, but for completion of such a far-fetched plan, you have to have the follow through that only comes with a bunch of buddies having downed a six pack or two of brew. They pilfered the scaffold from a jobsite of someone they knew really wouldn't mind. They loaded it on a 1958 International Harvester early in the morning, and by late morning, they were transferring it to the johnboat. It was all a matter of balance and beer to get out to the bar.

As luck would have it, it was a smooth morning, glassy and calm. Sometimes, the Gulf of Mexico looks like a serene, peaceful lake. The metal frames rode easily on the boat, and then it was just a matter of placing them. The reality is, that it's really only six or seven feet deep at the second bar. After the first section is dropped into the sandy bottom, then it was a simple job to feel the cross braces into their slots. It got easier, because, by the second stage of scaffolding, the "tower" was rising above the water. They probably went up a couple more stages, getting maybe ten feet above the water, and then it was simply a matter of getting the coolers and the fishing poles up the ladder to the top.

The guys got baked that afternoon, no doubt. No one really has a definitive answer as to if they caught a damn fish or not. But, I'm willing to bet, they watched a gorgeous sunset, and they added another chapter to the possibilities of what really went on in South Walton in the seventies.

Message In A Bottle

It was a day like any other day, except that I was going to tackle a job I had managed to put off for years. I had built my house on a hill overlooking Eastern Lake about three years ago. The house was built on a clearing on top of the hill, but the hillside itself was a jungle of scrub oak, palmetto, holly bushes and all manner of vines and entanglements. During the construction, I had blazed a path down the hill with machete and hatchet and had built a small winding set of primitive stairs. At that time I had noticed a line of debris in the dense foliage that stuck out like a sore thumb. There were pieces of Styrofoam, beer cans, and a miscellaneous collection of annoying pieces of plastic that interrupted the natural beauty of the wilderness hillside. But it was so dense and difficult to penetrate that I had successfully put it off all these years. I was fairly sure the junk had been there from the storm surge of hurricane Opal in 1995 and I was sure it wasn't going anywhere unless I did something about it.

I put on my oldest boots, my worst jeans, an old sweatshirt, and gloves, and plunged in, crawling around and thru the twisted limbs, until I got to the center of the debris line. I started picking up pieces of stuff, almost all of them pieces of colored plastic, brittle, yet enduring. These pieces of toys, these Styrofoam cups and cooler lids, these aluminum beer cans. These things seemed to be the lasting remnants of human civilization that had washed up on my hill. This was all that could be said for the humans that had walked this beach before: they were a bunch of litterers.

I picked up a bottle or two in the bunch, but then one of them caught my eye. It had a cork still in it. It had some piece of paper in it. As I gazed through the glass the letters M-E-S-S-A-G-E 1983 appeared to me. I was stunned. I rushed the bottle into the house and when my wife got home, we set about trying carefully to remove the cork. Some water had managed to creep into the bottle, so we had to be careful, but at the same time we had to be swift, so that no more damage could happen to the note. Of course we were dying with curiosity. Was it a treasure map? Where did it come from? Who wrote the note? We were giddy with questions.

After some struggle we were able to free the paper from the bottle and carefully unfold it. In its entirety, it read:

7-21-83
Lat. 14 degrees 30minutes N
Long. 81 degrees 30 minutes W
San Andreas

Hey,
What better way to celebrate the end of this bottle than to send it off to sea and eternity w/ the tides? Where it ends up...who knows? Contact me at:
A.A. 2138
Manizales, Colombia   S.A.

My name is Michael Klink. I'm principal of a school in Manizales. Hey, it's lucky to find a message in a bottle. No treasure though, eh?
—Mike

Then my thoughts began to wander and I couldn't help but picture this bottle bobbing on the ocean, millions of waves just lapping over it. I could see the bows of huge ships carve wakes that cut past the bottle, pushing it farther somewhere. I could see the bottle tossed in storm after storm. I could see it laying on the surface of the Gulf for days upon days. The bottle slept lifeless until one fateful night it became captured in the storm surge of Hurricane Opal in the middle of October 1995. It was pushed ashore, one speck of debris in the tons and tons of flotsam and jetsam that washed ashore that night. The debris was literally chest deep on the lakeshore, that morning. It stayed there for weeks as scavengers picked out the best parts of it. Deck boards and posts and light fixtures would be salvaged. My old aluminum Grumman canoe somehow made it through intact. But in the end, the county had to send in a bulldozer and four dump trucks to carry away the mess from the Eastern Lake shoreline All of it, except the pieces and parts that got pushed deep into the scrub oak and palmetto. It was there that the bottle slept, half buried in the sand and soil, with just a couple of spoonfuls of water that had seeped inside in the twenty years since it had left Mike's hand.

And now I wonder about the person who cast this bottle to the ocean. He must have been a dreamer on a Caribbean vacation. San Andreas is an island off the shore of Colombia. With a name like Klink, he was surely not a native, but just how long he lived in Colombia was the biggest mystery before me. It's a long shot I just have to take to try to write him and send a letter via airmail, with almost no chance to track him down after the many thousands of miles he has journeyed since San Andreas, July 21, 1983. But it seems so simple compared to the journey the message in the bottle has taken from that day to Seagrove, Florida, January 10, 2004.

THIRTY-THREE 'CHUTES

And it came to pass that the last flight of planes would go out on July 4th, in the late afternoon. There would be thirty-three jets all together, all of them F-16's. They were the last of the jet fighters, the once awesome symbol of America's military madness, and now these incredibly powerful and lethal machines would fly their last sortie into the Gulf of Mexico. The whole thing was a public relations stunt, but truly a beautiful one. In these last few months of the Universal Disarmament Program, people from both the Kremlin and the Pentagon had become so euphoric, so satisfied that it was really working, that they had become ever more theatrical, even playful, in the way they went about the letter and the spirit of the treaty: the destruction of all weapons.

We were sitting in our lawn chairs on the bluff overlooking the beach, sipping on cold beers from the cooler as we had done every 4th of July, but this was truly unique. The excitement and the joy in the air were truly intoxicating. Everybody was grinning and sometimes hugging, even the Colonels and Generals, who were acting absolutely silly, wearing things like plaid Bermuda shorts with their Air Force caps on backwards.

And the crowd must have been in the thousands, all poised on the beach for the last fly-by. An entire flotilla of fishing boats cruised purposely off shore. Surfers played in the waves, as if this were just another day.

And then they came roaring down on us like so many screaming banshees. They were awesome in their power and grace, yet they were the very incarnation of evil. Thirty-three F-16 Phantoms came shrieking out of the north at treetop level all in one wide wave heading out to sea to the cheers of the crowds, many of whom, even the surfers were saluting as they swigged their beers.

The formation, almost as one, barrel-rolled, climbed to two thousand feet, and then, in unison, all the pilots ejected. Thirty three 'chutes popped happily into view as the last of the fighter jets spiraled inevitably to their watery graves. The fishing boats sped quickly to pick up the hero pilots, dousing them with champagne as they pulled them on board. On the shore, we simply hugged and cried for joy. No one left the party 'til the last wink of the sun slipped into the sea.

HARD WAY HORN

"'Hard Way Horn' they call me," my dad kind of grinned and tapped his noggin, as he went about his work. He was laboring on building his sailboat this particular day, but I remember him using that phrase from time to time, poking fun at the way he would tackle a problem. Just using his own ingenuity and hard work rather than rely on anything or anyone else. No tricks, no shortcuts. I took it as a source of pride. I inherited much from him and this tendency to figure things out on his own, and to shy away from shortcuts and fast fixes was especially true. In carpentry, and probably in life as well, the hard way was usually the right way. There doesn't seem to be many things of worth that do not take hard work and determination rather than short cuts and clever tricks.

I also liked to prepare things: cut a lot of pieces, have them ready, then assemble them in one fell swoop, and make it seem like it all came together with magic. It was really all hard work and planning. It's enjoyable to work towards an outcome. And have reliance on the fact that all the little trials and tribulations that you have to endure for your craft, will eventually pay off in a fine, finished piece of achievement. There will be times when you say to yourself, "what have I gotten myself into?" But if you remember the spark that led you to start this thing, and simply stay persistent in trying day by day to achieve it, it is a glowing feeling to be able to just sit back and look at what you have done.

The cleverness lasts but moments. The flashes of brilliant imagination are grand but fleeting. After days or even months of work, you generally have a sagging of spirit, but then you have to wipe the sweat from your eyes, mutter "Hard Way Horn" once again, and just carry on.

THE LAKEHOUSE

October 23, 2000: A major milestone: When the fireplace stopped floating around in my brain, and the windows came to rest, I knew I had come close to having my house designed. Before this time, I still could not find just the right spot for the fireplace and there were just a multitude of places to put the windows. But now I had seemed to find the best place for them. And, it was about time, since there were about ten big black guys digging big trenches in my dirt. These trenches would be the concrete footers for my foundation, and no doubt, my house had begun. After two years of planning, and re-drawing, and wads of crumpled paper where the rooms just didn't work right, it was simply time to start the house. The papers had stacked up with tons of intellectual detail, but now the house was soon becoming concrete, literally.

As May pulled to a close, the house came to a major milestone: the installation of the circletop picture window. It was truly when the windows came to rest. For months the windows had been swirling around in my brain. All the difficult changes and framing decisions had been hammered into shape. The irony of the window was the timing. It went in at the beginning of the new moon, the darkest part of the month. The irony was that the major part of the entire design of the house was to catch the rising moon across the lake. The morning sun was by this time a harsh relentless reminder of the drought we were in. It would be weeks before the vistas I had imagined might align. As I reminisced, it became clear it was a house for all seasons. It had started out as a rainy, soggy adventure, with rainstorms literally every other day during the beginning month. Then came the days of cold; deep frigid mornings when I had bundled myself against the winter's blast as I started to stand the walls.

One particular morning, when it was too darn cold to really get started, I tried to warm myself by cleaning up the mess that was constant on the jobsite. Fully half the job itself was the constant cleaning up of construction debris. I did all the chores myself, managing to get the place neat and tidy for maybe one Sunday afternoon until I messed it up again Monday thru Friday. This particular cold, cold Monday I was trying to shovel the pile of sawdust I had swept together a couple days before, and was stunned as the shovel clunked against the pile. The sawdust not only had a patina of frost on it, but it was frozen solid! In twenty odd years of working in all conditions, I could not remember any frozen sawdust. Some mornings were so cold that, even with gloves, my fingertips would ache so bad, I was forced to retreat to another cup of coffee back at the trailer.

But now it was late May, and the drought had kicked in with brutal heat and a relentless sun beating down, and the retreat was to a tiny envelope of air-conditioning that was "The Camper," 144 square feet of living space, just enough to sleep, pee, make coffee, and tap away on my computer. The phone line was run through a window with duct tape for weather-stripping. I had to go out each evening and light the hot water heater manually because the pilot light would not work right. I slept on a two-inch foam mat not much different than the accommodations in most local jails. Needless to say, I had no cable TV. Life in the camper was getting to be a drab routine, sparked by incidents of ants, leaks, constant sand infiltrating the bed sheets, mud, unruly water heater, or a combination of everything that could go wrong on a camping trip. One hasn't experienced true camping until, first thing in the morning, one puts on a pair of underwear that a host of ants have decided to make home. I was completely covered in them, but three of them made their presence known in precious places, before I had a chance to even open my eyes.

Bedtime came early and the mornings came even earlier. Where had the springtime gone? It was a swirl of chaos: plumbers, electricians, and AC men. It was battling the elements to get the plywood on the roof, and then roofing it, and it had yet to rain, since it'd been "dried-in."

I remember cutting in the roof to be a very arduous task. I used twenty-foot pressure treated two-by-twelves for the rafters and cut the tails by myself. I had my buddy, Fred, to come help me when it was time to stand the ridge. The two of us spent nearly an entire day just moving these extremely heavy timbers up onto the second floor and through the existing framed partition walls. Fred, straining and cussing, remarked it was like "wrestling trees." Later, when we were trying to swing them up and position them against the ridge, it became more like "dancing with trees." There is a certain finesse in the way a carpenter has to move to get the pieces he is playing with into the places they have to fit. Sometimes you have to move with the grace of a dancer more than with the strength of a mule. Sometimes, I imagined myself as the Michael Jordan of carpenters, with strength, finesse and dexterity, with all the right moves. Most often, it just came down to perseverance. Anyway, Fred and I got the rafters up and his buddy Dave got out of jail at just the right time to give us much needed help getting the plywood up and the roof dried in.

Through all of this, I had changed my mind so many times as I tried to place the windows in just the right places. I was totally winging it. Some windows, although already ordered and in storage, were eliminated, and others were moved. One or two new ones were ordered and some I was able to change out for a different size. Anyway, the windows had finally come to rest, and the house was finally "designed."

Midway through the process, I began to feel nostalgia of sorts. I remembered the first weeks of the framing, when everything was laid-back. No time schedule; just building walls, gradually, day by day. I remember the very first day when the slab was first poured, November 11th, the year 2000. I stood on this big blank gray slab of concrete, and one of the first thoughts I had was that this was my toy, my great big adventure in doing what I wanted to do, what I had been practicing to do for over two decades, what I'm really good at. This was destiny and a grand challenge. There was a strange sense that there really was no hurry, no stress involved in getting it done as soon as possible. There would be stress down the road, I'm sure, but now I had money in my pocket and a big blank slab. Of course, there was a vague awareness that I was fully committed to this. No matter what happened, I would have to see this through to completion.

Now, it was the latter part of the framing, it was the time of decisions and number crunching; of relentless worrying about minute details and nooks and crannies. Not to mention really difficult problems. All the problems, I had to keep in mind, were of my own doing. The house simply got complex because it was never completely visualized and drawn out to begin with. I simply did not know what I would want, until I started to build the thing. It unfolded in a way that made me go back and make ever more constant changes, which weren't really refinements as much as creative alternatives to constantly keep myself from being painted into a corner, carpentry-wise. It was very much a mirror image of my quirky mind. So basically, it was as inefficient as a house could be built, with me tearing out and redoing major portions of partition walls and constantly adding more blocking, more blocking.

But now, as I lay down on the couch on the first night in the new house and looked up at the kitchen ceiling, it looked so good. It looked brand new to me. Although I had installed the v-groove pine ceiling perhaps eight or nine months ago, it had been something I had never much paid attention to, since the last coat of varnish. It was only now that I could lay back and realize that the vision I had so many years ago was valid. The effort I had put into it so many months ago was now paying off in the solid, warm feeling of a house well-built. Almost every aspect of the house resonated the same way. At the time that I was doing the work, I was very much wrapped up the strife and stress of just trying to get it finished. There seemed to evolve so many unforeseen obstacles. This was an incredibly complex and complicated house. Details were not thought out, so I was forced to improvise a great deal. The ideas were never on paper but forever bubbling in my head. But now there was a certain peace that the task was finished as well as it could possibly be done. It was now the time for the fun stuff: installing curtains, clothes rods, towel bars. All the little things that make living in a home comfortable. We were even thinking of hanging some of the pictures, although it will be tough to endure the pain when we drive that first nail into the sheetrock.

Scrub Oaks

I think my trees are smarter than me. If fact, they just may be the smartest trees in the whole wide world. That's because my trees are dwarf live oaks, a particularly prevalent species of tree found in Seagrove, often referred to as Scrub Oaks. I built my house in a large, wide grove of scrub oaks, and I have been dealing with them ever since.

The reason they seem so smart is that they just don't interfere with me, or my house, enough for me to ever have to take them out. They grow in a twisted way, with branches that seem to sprout out of nowhere and amble off sideways to almost anywhere they can find the light.

In the building of my house I was truly staggered by the volumes of tree branches I had to cut, and then further staggered by the amount of time and energy I had to put into collecting and disposing of the limbs and branches. It became a full time job in itself.

But did all my trimming stagger these trees? No way. They just kept branching out in their curious, twisted way, and they seemed to leave me and my house alone for many years. Pretty smart, huh? A normal oak would have grown straight up with big roots that threatened my foundation. A pine tree would have grown up feeble, like most of them along the coast, and just become an eyesore. I guess the pine tree was never meant to be a beach dweller.

The scrub oak was simply made for the beach environment. The spindly branches bend and sway in even the toughest winds, and never break. In fact, I consider them to be my armor against the tropical storms. They sway and twist, in a frenzied mass, as the winds reach past the seventy-five mile per hour point, and yet there is a certain calmness at the base of them. You are enveloped in a dome of leaves and branches that deflect the brunt of the storm overhead. If I was surrounded by pine trees, I would be scared that they would lose their grip on the earth, and come crashing on my roof. My scrubs are just so smart. They keep their grip, no matter what.

Of course, they can be a little bit mischievous. I mean, they drop their leaves in the spring instead of the fall. What's up with that? And then there are the "pollen pods". Every year, usually about the middle of May, they grow new, beautiful little bright green shoots of new leaves and tiny small branches. It always warms my heart. And, about the same time, they produce these golden strands of pollen, which we refer to as the "worms." They seem to fall in one big day, and blanket the entire yard in a golden haze. It can be quite beautiful for a day or two, but then it becomes a nuisance that must be dealt with. Out comes the rakes, brooms, and garbage bags.

I suppose I treat my trees somewhat like pets. They need a fair amount of trimming and training, a bit of maintenance here and there, but they seem to return the gestures with shelter, shade, and love.

EPISODES OF AN EXTRA

December 2nd: The first day's weather came out like a gem. It was a grand, shining, sunny day in Seaside. It was time for the carnival to begin. Paramount Pictures was about to begin the test shooting of The Truman Show. I was set in my position at the Holl Building. I was more than a little apprehensive of what the day was going to bring. We were beginning the re-roofing/renovation of one of the most important buildings in Seaside, the first major building, and one of the busiest buildings going on there. I was quite nervous and excited about the job. It was an important place to be and, quite frankly, I loved the challenge. All this was going through my mind as I drove into Seaside this morning, and then I rounded the corner and there were the trailers. This was Paramount Pictures camped all around me. And I was starting the most ambitious two months of my life.

The actual movie people had arrived. All these weeks and weeks of construction, of sets being built and painted and stocked. All the new bushes and trees being planted, some of them fake. All the Preparation was merely prelude. Prelude to the circus. And now the trailers were here. Six of them were camped all about the Holl Building. There were two dozen more of them surrounding the Lyceum, I would find out later. There I was, in this post-modernist castle gazing down from the parapets at the hordes of Hollywood below. But, actually, they were just like regular people. Perhaps just a little better looking than average. Perhaps just a little more organized and high tech. I've never seen so many walkie-talkies and cell-phones. Everybody seemed to be tuned in. It seemed like everybody was talking to somebody over the airwaves and it all seemed so important. You could pick out the director rather easily. He had the coolest hat, not to mention the cool, serene demeanor that relayed a sense that he was quite in charge. All the others came to him with reports and questions and it just seemed like the movements of all the equipment, the camera and the camera crews just cruised along like well-oiled machinery. On one side of my castle, was the film crew, setting up large white screens and running cable, all so smoothly. On the other side of the building, the sets were in their finishing stages with painters adding final touches to the columns, some of which now had been painted four or five times, each time with a different faux finish and each time in different hues. The concrete guys were everywhere trying to install the last pieces of steel that criss-crossed all the sidewalks that had been poured simply for this movie. They still had to paint various pieces of the concrete to resemble the famous Seaside red brick roads. They seemed far from finished, considering that filming was to begin in about five days. Little did I know.

But the town itself, in its entirety, was looking finished. I had been watching Seaside since its beginnings, watching it grow, gaining satisfaction in my own small contribution to its formation, and it seemed, as always, that Seaside was ever-expanding and evolving. Now it was taking on a whole, huge new feeling of being "complete". Although many of the buildings surrounding the town center were fake, impeccable facades created in weeks by the Paramount wizards, from the lofty havens of the "B-units," off the west side of the Holl Building, one could see the vast vision of the complete Seaside, and it was truly awesome.

Sometimes it takes an event like the circus coming to town to make us realize just how great this town has truly become, and it's still becoming more each day.

Back to December 2nd, 1996: On one side, the construction advanced toward completion, on the other, the film and make-up people had just begun to weave their separate crafts together, efficiently setting up and then waiting for that last special ingredient, the players. I was walking down Quincy Circle, on my way back to Ruskin Place, to the work trailer and the other project I was also involved in, when I first got a glimpse of Jim Carrey. I was captivated by the way he was dressed: an absolutely perfect tweed jacket with contrasting vest and matching trousers, and the absolutely coolest two-tone hush-puppy shoes I have ever seen. The outfit was a brownish-tan sort of plaid with bits of burgundy and a burgundy bow tie to set it off completely. When he turned to walk down the road to the temporary set, I saw that his jacket was pulled tight in the back with safety pins. And even that seemed cool. Welcome to make-believe. Other than that, Jim looked like just an average guy, somewhat dazzled himself by these ideal and surreal surroundings. Although he didn't noticed me, I think I caught him casting a wondering eye at my construction site, Castle Holl, and I was proud.

December 3rd: Seaside was fast becoming Seahaven. The street signs were being changed to cover all references to Seaside. It's now The Island Bank and Trust rather than Shades. It's Omnicom, a seven story building, after computer enhancement, where just a clump of shrubs had been, just a week before, and, perhaps, for a hundred years. There were new sculptures, awnings, etc. It was getting more difficult to remember what was Seaside and what was not. And who cares! I've had to try to stop keeping track of how many times I've seen Jim. I guess it will just get commonplace. Now, Dennis Hopper is a different matter. If he came to town, I would probably gawk and perhaps try to say hi! Who knows?

Later that day, I quickly get a haircut to be just right when my part is up. Oh, I forgot to tell you, I'm going to be an extra! It is just like the circus coming to town. In one more week, it's Showtime! I wore my "cool hat" to work, but I wore it only because it was windy and my hair was getting in my eyes. I swear I have not gone Hollywood, yet.

December 9th, 1996. It's Monday and they haven't called. The shooting is supposed to happen in the town center on Wednesday, and they haven't called! I'm getting nervous. Enough so, that I called them and they just say: we'll call you. How embarrassing. And it isn't just a well-worn cliché... they will call you.

December 10th. They do call! Come in at 5 a.m. Wednesday, at the Christian International Church. They called me at about 6pm and I had to think about trying to get to sleep early and yet I was so nervous, I really didn't sleep much at all.

December 11th, the Big Day, started early as I awoke at about 3:10, and lay in bed until the alarm screeched in at 3:20. I took another shower even though it was probably 10pm, just five hours ago, when I had taken my last shower. Oh well, can't be too sure. Got to be ready.

I got to the church almost 15 minutes early, but it was only a parking place to catch the bus to Seahaven. Even the bus had the logo. It was one of those small buses, perhaps 25 or 30 people, and I was one of the last people on, so I had to walk to the very back, and I thought I was in heaven! Perhaps it was the pre-dawn numbness of sleep deprivation, or perhaps the subdued atmosphere of a brand new bus in the middle of the night that made it seem so surreal. Every other person on the bus seemed to be a beautiful woman. Almost all seemed to be blondes, and we were about to embark on a trip to a fantasy town disguised as a movie set or was it a movie set devised as a town? It was both, and it was indeed getting to seem unreal.

Not all the gals were blondes. In fact there was a quite attractive brunette in the back right seat and I was one vacant seat away from her until another good-looking girl was forced to sit in back also, so I neighborly scrunched to the right. So there I was, between two beautiful women in a Disney-like dimly lit bus full of excited people. This was not too bad.

We got to the tent city in ten minutes and it was time to sign in. It started to feel a lot more army-like. I'm not sure I ever felt as lame as when I was trying to read the application card in a dimly lit tent at 5:30am, without my reading glasses! A sweet girl across the table had to tell me where to sign and where to make my marks. It was silly. I signed my name probably five times on something I couldn't even read.

After that it was to wardrobe to get our clothes, and to the dressing tent. In a manner of minutes all the guys around me were transformed into suit-wearing businessmen and it seemed like I was the last "tourist" alive. The fact that I have been living in Florida for over 33 years and I am now being officially labeled as a tourist, this is weighing heavily on my irony scale. Actually, there were several of us "casuals", as I chose to call us, either shoppers or tourists. And I think vendors could have been put in our group. We were clearly not businessmen and businesswomen, nor were we cops, greens keepers, nor fishermen. We were tourists, all in all, and proud of it. There were cops, and fishermen, and maintenance men and bus drivers and joggers, but a vast majority of the extras, or "background" as they called us, were businessmen. We soon moved on to "make-up", which was three chairs in the back of the big tent, with several rather confused looking hair-cutters, who I guess had never before cut 250 customers at six in the morning in a dimly-lit tent in Seaside er.. Seahaven. I really didn't much fret about my haircut, since I was going to be wearing my hat. I had discovered a rather cute, smallish, Indiana Jones sort of hat at Wal-Mart and it had passed through wardrobe and now I felt cool. Perhaps I had gone a little Hollywood. Perhaps it was the hat. I had become the hat. Or the hat had possessed me. Or perhaps, it was just a hat.

The haircut proved to be the last exciting thing to happen for the next two or three hours. It would soon become a matter of just waiting and hanging around, but there was quite a nervous excitement about it. The whole atmosphere seemed to be like attending a wedding reception of a distant tea-totaling relative. I encountered about a half dozen people I knew, and I, slowly but surely, met maybe a dozen more new strangers. And, after a couple of hours, I was ready to go. But we couldn't leave. Perhaps it was like a pleasant, co-ed work camp. We just sort of hung-out and occasionally ate doughnuts and coffee.

There were occasional speeches by the crew that were handling us. There were occasional trips outside. For instance, one time they called for all the "shoppers and homeless" to go to "props" which was a truck where they handed out bags of boxes to the shoppers, mostly the women, and a shopping cart for the "homeless guy." There seemed to be only one homeless guy in Seahaven. He was the one with the longest beard. The other two bearded guys were fishermen with their plastic lobsters. A substantial majority were businessmen and businesswomen, all in suits, and it seemed like everyone had a briefcase. Businessmen to the left, businesswomen to the right. But there I was in the middle being casual, if not downright tourist. I simply tried to keep an eye on the other "shoppers" so I wouldn't miss the call.

Sometime about eleven we finally were called. I went out into the

Seahaven town square with about a dozen other tourists. By now it was getting rather fuzzy as to whether I was a tourist or a shopper. They put me and two other gals in front of the Seahaven information sign, and that was to be my Spot. Twice the AD (assistant director, who would later become Jonathan) drove by in a golf cart imitating a camera, and that was that. It was back to the tent for lunch and more standing around.

December 16th: Our second day of "shooting" was about like the first. The day started off with blue skies, but gradually deteriorated. The wind came up, the clouds rolled in, the temperature dropped. It seemed a lot like being in the army, except that everybody was so well dressed. Beautiful women were scattered here and there, all dressed so fine in their business suits. It didn't help my spirits much when all these business people were being called for all these fill in shots. There still was not enough sunshine for the big town center circle scene, which I was supposed to be in. The day really was quite miserable. It was capped off by the casting director asking for volunteers to play a beach scene, with possible swimming, on Christmas Eve day. Off course I stood in line for that. I believe I'm starting to get desperate to get into this film. One of my "tourist" cronies said he just happened to be watching the deli scene which was supposed to be just businessmen and he was called to be in the shot. I guess I'm just not hanging around in the right way. Creative loitering seems to be way to go.

December 18th. We are called in after being canceled because of rain on Tuesday. It seems somewhat clear, but they dismiss us and give us a half day. I come home and crawl back into bed, very grateful. It rains all day long.

December 19th, Thursday. It's so cold as I'm walking to the tent from my truck; I have to turn myself away from the wind. It's so cold. Many of the old familiar faces have dropped out. There are a few new faces, flush with eager anticipation. They'll soon learn. I'm bundled up, big time, but it barely helps. We are taken out to our original spots early and then we cower in the shops because it's incredibly cold. The wind slices right through us. Even the casting directors are mumbling about how insane this is. Everybody is bundled up so you can't tell what sort of costume they are. Again, the business people seem to be called for all the shots, but at least we get to watch the process in action, and now I know why it takes so long. Quite by accident, I find the sweet spot. A few of the extras are waiting in a small school bus parked on the set. It is truly warm and situated with a perfect close-up view of the current scene being shot. We are close enough to see Jim Carrey's world famous dimples. I actually get to walk through a scene for two seconds, with Jim less than twenty feet away. My "date" and I do the scene twice with much shivering and freezing in between. Just as I'm thinking all this might be worth it for those two seconds of showtime, they run the scene two more times with groundskeepers instead of me and my "date." I hear the sound of my character splattering on the editing room floor.

December 20, Friday. Although it's absolutely cold, so cold, it ain't so bad. I find out that the wind chill was zero yesterday and that the temperature and wind chill will be a much better today, probably in the twenties. I'm so happy. We're veterans now. Everybody dresses practical. No strange blend of gloves, overcoats, and sweatpants seems the least bit absurd. There's one guy who wears a blanket that looks like a bear suit and he stands there all day looking like a woolly mountain. And we admire him. He just looks warm.

This is day two of the new recruits. A lot of people dropped out after the first awful cold wave. I don't blame them. This job is severely demeaning and absurdly freezing, and, if it weren't for the camaraderie, it would surely be hell. It's simply being together in a silly, frivolous endeavor that actually motivated us to be here in the first place, even before the cold front. Did any of us take this seriously to begin with? Check your sense of humor at the door.

The subplots of our drama begin to unfold these last couple of days. The tall beautiful blonde who just looks like an actress is forever being seen in the presence of the tall maintenance man. So much so that everyone thinks they are married. I find out later they are not married. She is seen constantly in the company of a businessman in the coming weeks. One of the new recruits has been dubbed "sweet cheeks." Although she does have an incredibly cute face, I suspect they are talking about the way she fills out the jogging tights she has been wearing most proudly. I doubt there is one person in the cast or crew who hasn't taken notice of her. She is definitely making her presence known. My friend, the bus driver, has dropped out. My friend, the bartender, is gone. The statuesque, elegant businesswoman has left. I don't blame them much. It is absurd and demeaning, but again, the camaraderie is fun, and watching filmmaking up close is really unique. There's another guy who looks like my bartender friend. There is also a guy who looks like Dennis Quaid. And isn't that Meryl Streep, and Tim Matheson, and Bonnie Bedelia, and, maybe, John Madden, and, maybe, I've been here way too long.

Besides chitchat, doughnuts, and imagining celebrity look-alikes, we pass some of the time watching the movie being filmed. The whole complicated, involved process seems to be a crew of perhaps fifty technicians, artists, directors, assistant directors, and assistants to the assistants, lighting people, assistant lighting people, and on and on, trying to locate the right spot. The director and the cinematographer seem like two kindly wizards, wise beyond their years, who have been studying human interaction for a lifetime. They instinctively know how people move and what they do with their gestures and words. They study the sky, the clouds, the buildings, the light, and somehow pick the perfect location to place their "many-jeweled device," the camera, with just the perfect lens, the perfect filters, the perfect reflectors, collectors, deflectors, the perfect angle, and then attempt to blend in the perfect flow of "background" (that's us). And bring it all together to be poised for the essential element, the "actors."

All this takes time. And all we do is wait and shake. Occasionally we are herded and separated into groups by the P.A.s (production assistants). The P.A.s, or handlers as I chose to call them, all have on headsets, and often look very absorbed in conversations we know nothing about. We are told to walk here and there on cue. No major directions needed. "Walk there, look happy, look warm. Don't shiver, don't scrunch." When everything's ready, Jim the Star appears from somewhere. It's still impossible to see exactly where he stays during most of this. Then someone yells, "rolling... Background!" and it's our golden moment. We do our job, which is mostly just walking, and then Jim does his job, and the whole thing comes together for about forty seconds, and then someone yells, "Cut." We all scurry to find our coats and sweatpants. And Jim, I suppose, goes back to his heated trailer.

This happens again and again. And that's on a good day. Sometimes we wait for four or five hours just for those thirty or forty golden seconds. Some days, a majority of the hours are spent hanging around the tent waiting for the weather to break. There would have been more diversions for me, perhaps a romance to fantasize about, but virtually every gorgeous woman in the tent was married. I've never seen so many wedding rings in my entire life.

It really wasn't so bad. It's really rather neat to be put in this situation where it's absolutely normal to chitchat with everybody. You become, if not friends, then real good acquaintances, with literally hundreds of people. You joke around with total strangers. You stroll down the streets of Seahaven, smiling, with someone you'll probably never see again. But, you'll always remember these faces; you won't be able to forget these costumes. After seeing someone in the same clothes for over a month, won't they be bizarre in actual street clothes?

December 24th: It's actually quite mild weather-wise, but so absolutely boring. A lot of the old faces have dropped out, but there are some more new faces. One young lady has the most gorgeous eyes I have ever seen, but she is a student in college in Virginia. Most likely, she is half my age, and I really should grow up sometime. There seems to be more on-lookers, more civilians, as I call them, slipping into the crowds of extras that hang out, trying to catch a glimpse of the scene being shot. The production assistants kindly weed them out.

December 25th: Christmas comes and goes, almost without saying. I go by my job site early in the morning to check on things and Seaside/ Seahaven is beautifully deserted. Without people, I can intently gaze at the scenery and there are really some amazing views of this combination town. Breathtakingly pure vistas of a perfect little town. I walk through the deserted streets where days before there were energetic crowds of business people parading past the camera crews. I wonder now, if, every time I walk through Seaside, will it bring back visions of bicycling businessmen with their briefcases? I feel strangely unhinged from reality, but I suppose Seaside has always been like that to me.

Here it is, in the very last days of 1996 and I stand in the middle of this evolving experiment known as Seaside, surging proudly into the future, and, as the fog steals softly through the streets and avenues of my memory, I become immersed in the past...

January 6th, 1997: Call Time 4:30 P.M. It is a cold and miserable day with intermittent icy showers. This is to be our first night shoot. In the construction business, we often get behind schedule, and are always trying to catch up. Sometimes, when faced with a looming deadline, we joke about bringing in floodlights and working on through the night. Of course, we're just joking. In the movie business, they actually do it. Paramount pictures brought in a hundred foot long crane and mounted stadium-like floodlights that loomed over Seahaven like a cluster of brilliant full moons. The central square was like a football field. The towers of Ruskin Place stood like surrealistic sculptures against an ominous sky. It was cold and rainy, yet the show went on. The crews moved out with heavy, warm, raincoats, and comfortable, fashionable knee boots, their equipment wrapped in sheets of plastic, well-kept and tidy. We, the extras, the "background," trudged out like the huddled masses, yearning for freedom. Some of us wore blankets, some of us in sweatpants and over boots. All of us were truly cold. We were truly nuts now. Not a one of us was truly diluted into thinking this would be an easy night, an easy shoot. Little could we dream how bizarre it would really be. For over thirteen hours we did nothing but two things: We huddled freezing, muttering, and telling stupid jokes to pass the time; or we did the scene, over and over and over and over. We lined up, arm in arm with the same two people on either side, the same line of the same faces trailing into the cold night, and we march across Seahaven, searching with flashlights for Truman. We did this once, we did this twice, we did this not less than twenty five times with cameras moved and set from every angle. We did it a dozen times with "the dog" as the focus. The damn dog couldn't get his part right, I guess. We did it half a dozen times with the actors doing their lines. We watched four electricians using a $200 per hour forklift struggle to fix a lamppost, a task not much more difficult than changing a light bulb. It took them an hour. We did the scene in rehearsal all bundled in our overcoats and sweatpants. We did the scene with "coats off", that cruel, indecent, absurdity that we had all insanely volunteered for. We marched on, arm in arm, in Bermuda shorts and summer dresses, into the movies.

The truly insane thing was that we all came back the next night, January 7, 1997, and did it all again. It wasn't the same old arm in arm, but it was more "searching for Truman with flashlights." And it was bitterly cold. This time the shoot was in Ruskin Place and we were able to huddle in Cara Roy's shop for the indeterminable hours between shots. About fifteen of us just crashed out on the floor of her shop and spent our delirium in relative warmth. It was like a slumber party for grown-ups. The previous night had gone on a staggering thirteen hours. This night went only a merciful twelve.

Somewhere in these last couple of days, I managed about three hours' sleep and about five hours per day of work on my regular job. I don't recollect if I was able to bathe regularly in this time period. I don't recall much home life at all.

On Thursday, January 9, 1997, after a full day's work at my real job, I am headed home. I buy a beer and drink it on the way home. I am so glad to get home. I start a nice cozy fire. I dream of a nice, hot shower. I start to cook some chili as I open my second beer. A new episode of Seinfeld is coming on tonight and the couch looks like a bed of soft flowers to me.

The phone rings. It's Dana, from casting. Can you be down at the tent by 5:30 tonight? Sure, I mumble. I feel most definitely like a mindless zombie. But I just do it.

We wait around for about four hours with no food nor coffee. We feel quite used but what's new. About nine o'clock, they take us out to the highway and tell us to wade waist deep through the scrub oak with two flashlights looking for Truman. We have a deep suspicion that "Truman" is probably in a Jacuzzi somewhere in L.A. sipping a margarita, and counting his money. The whole scene begins to take on the atmosphere of a snipe hunt. Boy, do we feel foolish. They shoot the scene maybe three times, and then we go home. No food, no coffee. Movie making does not seem too glamorous at this point. I must admit when I first went to the casting call in mid-summer, I had delusions. I saw myself sitting at a table at an outdoor cafe, sipping champagne with a gorgeous starlet sitting opposite me. We sat and chatted and fell in love as the movie was shot all around us. I believe there were violins playing in my delusions. Now I have nightmares of wading through scrub oak in subfreezing weather with a twenty mile per hour wind cutting through me, and tyrannical assistant directors yelling "coats off."

The "snipe hunt" episode proves to be the last night shoot. Since Paramount has lost a few days because of bad weather, our schedule is even more misconstrued. They tell us day to day whether we will be coming back the next day. My real life job seems ever more distant. We actually get into a regular routine and put in a complete week from January 13 through January 16. The sixteenth is Jim Carrey's birthday. All the extras sign a card for him and it is rumored we would try to get together and sing "happy birthday" to him. It doesn't happen. He doesn't come by the tent either. As I'm strolling off across the Square after the day is done, I notice the crew is milling around the lunch truck and Jim is just hanging out on the side of the crowd. I start to move a little closer, and I see the Beast, Jim's bodyguard, eyeing me. I pretend to move on, then circle back, and the next thing you know, I'm standing next to the guy, saying, "Can I shake your hand?" He smiles that gorgeous smile, shakes my hand, and that is that. I remember that it's his birthday, and wish him "happy birthday, man," and I actually pat him on the back. Cool. He may not be Dennis Hopper, but hey, he's cool.

January 20, 1997. It's seems like another day on the set. Long hours of hanging out, but there's a feeling of finality in the air. It is rumored heavily that this will be our last day. "Sweater Guy" jokes that some of us will probably have to join Extras Anonymous: "Hi, my name's 'Indy' and I'm an incurable extra. I find myself walking over and over again into the Seven-Elevens until I get it right. If someone yells 'Rolling,' I immediately take off my coat and start strolling and grinning as if I'm in Seahaven. I'm incurable." We know we will surely miss these little get-togethers. Some of the gals have little guest books, and ask some of us to write something. It's just like signing a high school annual. I've almost got a crush on some of these women. The day drags on rather slowly. I feel like I have won some respect when at least two of the P.A.'s actually know me by name. But then, as we're checking out, they tell us that all but twenty of us are not going to be needed anymore. Most of us were caught off-guard even though we sensed it. There seemed very little time to say any silly good-byes much less exchange phone numbers. A sense of reality sets in that I probably wouldn't see but a handful of these people again, even if I had their phone numbers. This was just "so long 'til I see you on the silver screen." And that was also the reality. I would see many of them over and over again in the movie. And probably would see myself a couple times as well. It was quite a special time.

CONCERTS

I married a conservative woman, but it really has been wonderful. Since we are both in our early fifties, being somewhat conservative now seems to be just right. The only problem is that when I try to relate to her some of the wild liberal escapades of my youth, she just doesn't seem to be impressed. I'm talking mainly about the concert-going experience. I must warn some of you readers that the experiences of rock and roll concerts, and the experience of recreational drugs, are inevitably intertwined, so you'll just have to get used to it.

Also, going to a concert, and telling people about it (especially people who didn't get to see the groups you saw) is an act of coolness. I mean, telling my wife that I saw Pink Floyd in 1974, at the beginning of the Dark Side of the Moon tour, had absolutely no effect on her. She seemed to not know, nor care, just who Pink Floyd was. This was terribly deflating to me, so I'm telling my stories to you in the hope that maybe you'll be impressed.

My very first concert, I believe, was The Lettermen, sometime in 1970, I think. I know that's not that impressive, but you have to start somewhere. If you don't know who they were, just think "syrupy love longs." Man, what was I thinking? My first real rock and roll concert was Mountain. This was a greatly anticipated event. They had a big hit song, "Mississippi Queen," going on at the time, and we got to Tully Gymnasium in Tallahassee at least an hour and a half early to be the first ones in the door. This proved to be a bad move. Everything was fine at first. Me and several of my brother's surfer friends just hung out in front of the doors. But then we got bored and someone talked me into taking a little pink pill. Well, it didn't kick in until the crowd had gotten much larger. Soon, it wasn't so much fun with a music-starved crowd cramming us against the glass doors of the gym. This was really my first major experience of another feeling that usually goes hand and hand with concert crowds and drugs: paranoia.

Anyway, time seemed to stand still until they finally unleashed the doors and just a flood of people pushed us to a spot on the gymnasium floor, right in the front! I mean, we were about two or three rows back, sitting on a blanket, right in the middle. It was exhilarating. It was awesome, dude. And then the paranoia came right back. We were stuck in a sea of people, and how would we make our way out of this to get to the bathroom or get a coke? Sometimes the concert experience can be a survival trip. I'll never forget how stunned I was when Leslie West, the guitarist from Mountain, appeared on stage. I had pictured him as being a typical rock star, tall and handsome, but he was this big, fat, short guy, maybe five-foot-five, and at least three hundred pounds with frizzy hair. Hence the name: Mountain.

My next experiences were near misses. This is when you're such a dumb-ass that you miss a cool concert. You're not hip enough to know what the next cool thing is, and you miss it. O.K, I missed a chance to see The Allman Brothers, opening for Frank Zappa, just as they were getting hot. Through the years, at FSU in Tallahassee, there were some other names that played there that I had never heard of. Steve Martin was this goofy guy who use to play some local clubs, and then there was this guy Jimmy Buffet, but who would have ever thought they would amount to anything.

I did see Black Sabbath in those early days. They were something new and big at the time. I grew out of that fast. I remember they had an interesting opening band, somebody called Fleetwood Mac. A memorable moment in that show was when all the lights came on in Tully Gym during the show and the police escorted someone out. Man, talk about mass paranoia. Half the crowd almost peed in their pants.

Those first concerts in Tully Gym in my freshman year were done in what is called festival seating: no chairs, you just sat on a blanket on the floor. They changed that to seats (fold up chairs) later on, I think, for better crowd control. Me, and my buddy Bud, went to see Iron Butterfly with Blues Image, and sat in these seats. Our seats turned out to right next to this big ten-foot wide center aisle. So, when the lights went down, we simply scooted our chairs out into the aisle and had a completely unobstructed view for the entire show. We were such rebels.

Actually, I was still a beginner when it came to concerts until the summer after my freshman year, the summer of '70. Me and Reggie were just hanging out in Ft. Walton, bored with the same old scene, when we heard about the Atlanta Pop Festival. We didn't have any money, no car, and had no idea how much it would cost; we just knew that we had to go. We went down to Hardee's, the local hangout, and just started talking to people, hoping to beg a ride. Reggie was part con man, part silver-tongued devil. Miraculously, some of the first people we met were going up in two Volkswagen Beetles and they had room for us. It was so cool.

There was one snag: I was grounded by my parents that summer for an earlier party that had gotten out of hand. That was bad, but the good part was that they were going out of town that weekend. So

I just left them a note telling them that me and Reg were going back to Tallahassee to get a job for the summer. We just didn't mention that we were going thru Atlanta on the way. I guess, in effect, I was running away from home.

We left Friday afternoon. There were about six of us in the two Beetles. These people had food, sleeping bags, tents, plenty of pot, and somebody, probably Reggie, had some more of those little pink pills. About all we brought were our sleeping bags, a bottle of Southern Comfort, and one change of clothes. We had no idea what we were getting into.

Somewhere in Georgia, about ten o'clock at night, we were driving through a small town, when the blue lights began to flash. I remember this quite vividly because I had again taken one of those darn pills and I was just starting to feel a little loopy. A big fat Georgia sheriff's deputy had pulled one of us over for a loud muffler and the other car for following too close. He told the drivers we could stay in jail for about five days until the circuit court was convened, or they could pay the fine of about fifty dollars in cash right now. These people we rode up with were restaurant workers with a great sense of humor. They had most of their money in tip change, so they had their girlfriend sit on the pavement in front of the patrol car's headlights and count out fifty dollars in quarters that she poured out from a sock. The cop was fuming as we watched from the back seat of the car, trying our best not to laugh hysterically. It was so funny.

We headed on into the night and got on some interstate outside Roswell, Georgia. It must have been two or three o'clock in the morning but the highway was filled with cars just like ours: loaded with loaded people. It seemed like there was just a huge caravan of rock and rollers just grinning and boogying down the interstate into the night. Somewhere down the road, we turned off the highway and just started following the cars in front of us. No one knew if anyone knew where we were going. It was wild. So many people and cars and headlights and chaos. We kept following the cars in front of us, as they went down dirt roads and into fields and orchards and then we just parked where we could and threw out our sleeping bags and crashed where we were. There were tents and people in sleeping bags everywhere. It reminded me of a bivouac of soldiers from the Civil War. We were definitely a ragtag bunch.

When morning came we found out we were less than a hundred yards from the festival entrance. We were in the middle of a giant orchard filled with all manner of people camping in tents and vans and cars. People were sacked out on the hood of cars, under trees. There were bodies lying everywhere. There were people walking and laughing and dancing and playing Frisbee. I'm almost sure some of these people were smoking pot. I know I was. The good news of the day was that the festival was called a free festival. We wouldn't even have to hunt down a place to buy tickets. The bad news was there were so damn many people that, by the time we could round ourselves up and wander to the music area, we couldn't get much closer than a hundred yards from the stage. But that really didn't matter much. The real show was just the multitude and diversity of people. All kinds, all shapes, all colors. And everybody was just happy and high with anticipation.

The days were hot and dusty. It was July, and we were all sweaty most of the time. There were some makeshift showers with strictly cold water, but it seems like there were always long lines, so we mostly did without. We spent the days napping, sipping, smoking, and simply hanging out. The bands usually started playing around one in the afternoon and then there would be one after the other until one or two in the morning. It was an endurance test mostly. Napping and passing out became synonymous. It was increasingly hard to know what time it was, and it really didn't matter. We were either resting near the tents or making our way back towards the stage. It seems like most of the time we were making our way through the crowds, and making friends along the way. Sometimes, they would even share their Kool-Aid with us. I think that was a good thing. Somewhere in the fog we saw such bands as Spirit, Ten Years After, Jimi Hendrix, Jethro Tull, Santana, and a whole lot of bands that I just can't remember. Most especially we saw Grand Funk Railroad. Later, they would release a live album from their concert at Atlanta Pop Festival. Yep, that's me and Reggie yelling in the background, along with 500,000 of our closest friends.

If Atlanta was the high-water mark of my hippiedom, it certainly wasn't the end of my rock and roll era. At Campbell stadium in Tallahassee, I saw Ike and Tina Turner, Stevie Wonder, and Leon Russell, all in separate concerts. Leon was by far the loudest. I was front and center for that one and my ears were ringing for two days thereafter. The best I ever saw at Campbell Stadium was ZZ Top. They were on their Diablos tour, circa 1975, and they were known to have all manner of critters on stage, such as a longhorn steer, an armadillo, and a rattlesnake. FSU would not let them bring all those things into the stadium so they just showed up, with no stage decoration, almost no light show whatsoever, and just played. Three guys, one set of drums and two guitars, and yet they were the most awesome band I have ever heard. I saw Steven Stills there one winter night, but it was too darn cold, and you could tell he just wanted to get offstage.

Later on, they built a coliseum in Tallahassee, and I was able to see Talking Heads and Jimmy Buffet. Indoor coliseums have made the concert experience so much more comfortable and civilized, but I'll have to admit I was really, really paranoid trying to toke on a joint in the boy's bathroom. I miss the good old days of trying to hop the fence at Campbell Stadium and sneaking in. Designated seats also eliminated the elbow-to-elbow action of trying to squirm your way to a better position.

Paranoia played a different part in the largest concert I ever went to. It was in the Tangerine Bowl in Orlando. There were 63,000 people who had come to see The Who in the first show of their Farewell Tour 1993. Before we headed to the stadium, I thought I would prepare for the fest with a half-pint bottle of bourbon. I knew I would have to sneak it in, so I put it inside my boot. Just to make sure, and feeling so clever, I stashed a back-up bottle down the front of my pants. For added measure, I had about four joints rolled and ready in my front shirt pocket. You always wanted to have your pot handy in case you had to eat it very quickly. Anyway, we got to the stadium, and we were filing in, and it did not take the guys at the gate two seconds to spot my booze bottles and take them away. They just threw them into two large garbage cans full of liquor bottles. Anyway, they didn't find the pot on me, nor the other 50,000 rock and rollers who must have brought weed to the scene. When I looked around at the crowd during the concert, you could see at least ten joints being passed at any given moment. It was one big buzz.

As far as outdoor concerts go, the Beach Boys on the beach at Sandestin was the best. This was my crowning moment as far as sneaking into concerts. It was an afternoon show on a gorgeous hot summer day. I was too poor to pay the thirty-five dollars for a ticket, so I parked about a mile down the beach and walked down to where the show was set up. Unfortunately, they had a fence on the beach and security cops every so often. Fortunately, they couldn't run the fence into the Gulf. They simply had a line of buoys run out into the water cordoning off the fleet of boats and swimmers who had gathered for the party. I slipped my cooler and my pipe across the fence to a friend I found on the inside, and then waded out into the water. I watched the small waves breaking, and timed my move just right. At the proper moment, I took a huge breath, dove under the buoy line and swam with all I had. I wanted to make sure I got far enough inside the line so that the cops wouldn't see me, so I carefully surfaced in a cresting wave to catch another breath. Man, was I clever. I made it in to shore undetected and ended up front and center in a mass of suntanned, half-naked, partying people dancing to the sounds of "Fun, Fun, Fun" all afternoon.

Last, but not least, was the Pink Floyd concert in Jacksonville Coliseum. It was awesome. They are a phenomena rather than a typical band. The stage setting, the lights, the special effects, the sound: it gave you a feeling that Pink Floyd was some sort of "Entity," a surrealistic, omni-present machine, rather than a group of musicians, who seemed dwarfed by the entirety of the presentation. They were like small vessels thru which this extra-terrestrial power was channeled. Truly one of the greatest concerts of my life.

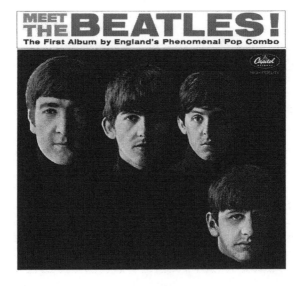

Formats

I bought an Ipod today. Yeah, I know it's been long overdue. I think I just have something against being pressured into taking on the next new technology against my will. I'm so tired of upgrading. But I must admit the Ipod is cool. I couldn't help but ponder the paths that my music has taken. The volumes and volumes of songs, and albums, and the many roads that these songs have taken, and now they all dwell in a capsule the size of a matchbook, and all I have to do is tap it, and these songs jump out across the decades.

My very first album was "Meet the Beatles," the Beatles first album. I was about thirteen years old, and my sister gave it to me for Christmas, 1963. That was all it took for me to get hooked. I, of course, ended up buying every Beatles album, every Doors album, every Pink Floyd album, and a multitude of others through the years.

These albums were made of vinyl, and were called LPs, for those of you too young to remember the good old days. I played these albums on my parent's hi-fi record player, a Grundig that my father bought while we were in Germany. It was sleek and cool, and sat in the living room next to our old oval-screen, black and white RCA television. Both of these machines were encased in beautiful wood consoles, and they were some of our most prized possessions. It would be pointless to try to remember the records I collected in those days. In the early days, it might have been the Buckinghams, the Grassroots, or Jan & Dean, but then later it became the Yardbirds, Spencer Davis Group, and Steppenwolf. I remember putting on the Doors' first album, turning off all the lights, and lying on the carpeted floor of that living room, with my eyes closed, and just yearning to embark upon the "Crystal Ship." I had borrowed that album from my buddy across the street from where I lived. You heard about new stuff from the radio, or perhaps seeing the new acts on TV, in such shows as *Shindig, Hullabaloo,* or *Where the Action Is.* I can't remember every album I ever had, but there were only two that I bought immediately the first time I ever laid eyes on them, without hesitation: The Beatles' *White Album,* and *Dark Side of the Moon.*

I remember listening to *Revolver* and wondering why it sounded so different, and, only later, realizing that it was my first album in "Stereo." This probably led to my first real record player, because, of course, I had to have separation. There was no way you could enjoy the frenetic orgasm that was at the core of "Whole Lotta Love" without putting your speakers on opposite sides of the room and feeling the music run from one to the other. My first true record player was a "suitcase," where the turntable folded down, and the speakers unhooked and extended maybe a dozen feet apart.

I took my suitcase and my albums with me when I went off to FSU. But, once I encountered other guys' collections and their superior turntables, it became obvious that I had somewhat abused my poor LP's. These guys at the frat house had Marantz receivers with diabolically precise turntables and Infinity speakers as tall as a dresser. These guys used cloths to clean their records, and sometimes even replaced the needles in their stylus. I couldn't compete.

And, anyway, something new came on the scene and prompted my first upgrade. I discovered cassettes. I knew I had absolutely no use for eight-tracks. I could never stand the "clunk" when it switched tracks, sometimes in the middle of a great song. And I knew I wanted to compile my own greatest hits and never have to listen to some of the clunkers on my favorite albums. I had found very few albums that had superior songs throughout. There always seem to be at least three of four songs I simply never wanted to listen to again. In those days I can only remember one album that didn't have a clunker, and that was "Abraxas."

So, I bought a small stationary cassette player/recorder and began to record my own greatest hits tapes. I very seldom bought a pre-recorded cassette. I was truly finicky about them clunkers. Eventually, I ditched my record player altogether and sold my albums for a dollar to anyone that would take them. In truth, they were badly abused and I probably just gave them away. The cassette player I bought was rather primitive and cheap, and I remember in its final days, I would have to sit it up on its side or else it wouldn't play correctly. When you ejected a tape, you had to try to catch it in mid-air.

About halfway through my college career, I found the crown jewel of all electronics I have ever owned. I can remember the shelf it was sitting on in the store. It was a Sony portable cassette player, what is now called a boom-box, but it was different. It was compact, sleek, and, most importantly, it had RCA jacks. No other boom-boxes, in that era, had this. From this moment on, it would be my loyal companion. The beauty of it was that I could take it with me anywhere, easily plug into my friends' amplifiers and record their stuff, as we sat around drinking and smoking, as we were wont to do in those days. I recorded many a rambling, disjointed, greatest hits tape in those days, and paid nary a dime.

Of course, there came a time when I had to acknowledge the onslaught of the compact disc, the CD. I was slow to embrace it because I had accumulated probably sixty or seventy cassettes of my favorite music, just the way I wanted them mixed. And then, of course, I was back to buying whole CD's, with no readily available way to make my compilations. I, of course, fell into the Amazon trap for aging baby boomers, and now could find all those lost albums of my youth with just the click of a mouse. After much complicated wrangling on the computer, I learned I could actually make playlists again. I actually found a service on line that converted a boxful of my old cassettes to CD's. I then downloaded the songs of these CD's into my computer. There were more than a few songs that had been recorded from LP to cassette (with scratches and pops, of course) then transferred to CD, then converted to MP3, and then, in the space of two minutes, all the music I had ever collected and saved for over thirty years, was placed into a tiny cube no bigger than a matchbox. Apple = awesome.

MOUNTAINFILMS

I tried to lie back the other night and remember the most vivid images of the Telluride Mountainfilm Festival. It was an inaugural event last November, in WaterColor, in which a group of people from Telluride came over here to put on a two night showing of their best and, I guess, latest documentary films. There were animations, action, travel, adventure...you name it. There was a bonfire, a wonderfully catered dinner, and a host of events and exhibits to entertain and inform people throughout the day. Kayaking, mountain climbing, and cross-country bicycling were just a few of the activities.

I was trying to pick my favorite, but I couldn't. The images of snow were everywhere. There was awesome footage of the raw power and breathtaking scope of avalanches. There was the mountain climbing, where the challenges and exhilaration of these men and women were brought very real to us. The mesmerizing, stunning shots of full-tilt snow skiing were every bit as exciting as the monstrous wave-riding and pure ballet of windsurfing. Each athlete seemed to be at the pinnacle of his sport.

There was an incredibly touching story about a monkey (who could ever forget Bobo, the greatest coconut fetcher in the south Pacific) and his wizened, old master and friend. This was just a great and moving insight into how people live with their surroundings on the other side of the globe. Wouldn't we all just love to have a Bobo?

"The Man Who Planted Trees" was as close to perfect visual poetry as anyone can get. It was a true story, a simple tale, done in excellent, impressionistic animation, that was about a man in the South of France, who simply took it upon himself to plant trees in a barren valley region, and, over time, he transformed it into a great forest, and changed the entire ecology of the area, so much for the better.

I will always be thankful for the airborne images of Patagonia and the lone saxophone playing pilot whose quest to find and record the places man has never been to. I can still see the most amazing glimpses of film where he had flown hundreds of miles just to approach those awesome mountain peaks for just a handful of moments. The solemn stoic beauty in his life's work is as wonderful as the images he has brought back for us. We were given a taste of just how personally satisfying it is to pursue one's own artistic vision, no matter how far it takes you.

That film was perhaps my favorite, I suppose, but the most satisfying and beautiful image of the entire pair of evenings were the stars. I must admit I didn't watch a great deal of the saga of the three African hunters. I got lost in the stars. There was something so comforting in gathering in a meadow with a tribe of casual coastal dwellers, well-equipped with their Woodbridge wine and Land's End lawn chairs, and simply laying on my back and staring at the nighttime sky. The temperature was perfect. The pine tree backdrop was perfect. The looming towers of the Boathouse, the Bathhouse, and the Baithouse were rustic reminders that this setting, this meadow, was simply a haven in the midst of an even larger "meadow," the overall evolving plan of WaterColor: a place where we can all have a part in planting our "trees."

I'm told Mountainfilm at WaterColor will be an annual tradition, and I'm quite sure, next year will be even better than this.

DAYDREAM EXTREME

Hampton sometimes took his daydreaming to extremes. One time, while painting one of his most simple constructions, a basic bench, a four by twelve slab of wood on two short posts, simplicity itself, he noticed how it resembled the symbol Pi, the ratio between the radius and the circumference of a circle. He saw a connection in this. It was a simple symbol, perhaps a bench of comfort or an elemental picture of shelter. But, it was also more than that. It was mathematical proof that there were relationships that were infinite. Isn't it somewhat comforting (and at the same time overwhelmingly awesome) that some things are infinite. Some "thing" which we call space does go on forever. Even if it is nothing but void space, it goes on forever! And the same has to be true for time as well. It is somewhat overwhelming, but at the same time reassuring. If time goes on forever (not just a long, long, long, long, long, long, long, long, long time but forever!) then all things will happen, everything will happen. It may take ten million, billion, quadrillion (and so on) eons, but something will evolve to the position of God, with all the power and responsibility that job includes. We can look out and see that space is infinite. We're pretty darn sure that time has to be, also. So, put the two together, and all things will eventually happen. Pi (an infinite relationship) is shelter.

THE POCKET

The best kept secret about living in Florida in the 30's (latitudes, that is) is the winters. The winters here last about a month, and are usually scattered over December, January and February, so that none of the cold can really pile up on you. There are weeks of autumn interspersed in there, as well as a splash of summer every once in a while. November comes in brilliant and clear with just a hint of cool breeze. Early December blusters in with several cold, rainy days but then it clears up, warms up, and you're back in "Florida" again. The sky can get so clear, a welcome change from the hazy steamy summer smother. The only clue that is it really winter is the silvery blue colors that reflect off the Gulf when the sun is lower in the midday sky. Sometimes Christmas can be shirtsleeve weather, but you can always drive to Grandma's in Tennessee if you miss the snow. January can start to get really cold for two or three weeks. If you live in an old Florida cottage, it can be exhilarating, if you know what I mean. I can remember one autumn night I went to sleep with only a sheet over me and sometime around midnight I felt a cold front come straight through the walls and I was sent clamoring though my closets in search of a blanket or two. The concept of insulation and central heating wasn't paramount to the builders of these early beach cabins.

If you have a wood burning stove, you are on the cutting edge of technology in some of these old houses. Chopping firewood by day, and stoking the cozy tranquil flames through the evenings, can be as romantic as a candlelight dinner, but when you dive into bed, you may need some survival training.

I think I have perfected what I call "the pocket," a technique for surviving, and perhaps, even enjoying the vigor of a cold winter night. I plunge under the covers, sometimes fully clothed. I curl up into a loose ball, with the blanket firmly secured beneath my chin. I pull a tuck of the blanket between my bony knees for padding, and slightly shiver until my body heat fills my little pocket. Then quickly, I pull my clothes off and jettison them from the envelope as fast as possible. The key to maintaining the pocket is to keep any motion to a minimum. Soon, I'm as cozy as can be.

Of course, like any other restless male, I often feel a need to toss and turn. In this situation, it must be a controlled turn. You must deftly heave yourself up, ever so slightly, perform a 180 degree turn just barely above the sheets, and, this is the key, land precisely in the same spot you were, which you have already warmed to perfection. Any miscalculation in this turn can bring you down onto portions of virgin cold sheets that can slap you awake, and then you have to start all over, warming your pocket.

This technique can be mastered by a solitary sturdy individual bent on saving utility bills, but can be complicated by the addition of a sleeping partner. While it seems to me, it would be quite difficult for two people to perform these maneuvers in tandem, I suspect that it really might be quite fun.

THE BUDDY SYSTEM

For everybody in Florida to really enjoy the beach experience, I think we need to use the buddy system. Teaming up with someone somewhat different than yourself opens up new worlds. In every beach town, there are those people known as locals. They, in general are a laid-back bunch. "Casual attire," for these guys, can be taken almost to an extreme. But lately I've noticed a new trend. Many of my buddies, who, in days gone by, would never have given up their flip-flops and cut-offs, are wearing shoes these days, sometimes wearing jeans. The most hideous thing of all, they now have cell-phones. They all have jobs. And that's really the crux of the matter. If you're living on the Emerald Coast, you're probably working too hard. You're probably zooming from job site to job site, muttering something about painters and drywall, all the time yakking on the cell phone and getting your daily nutritional requirements from Tom Thumb. This madness has got to stop, and I think I know the way.

You need to buddy up. You need to befriend a visitor (often mistakenly called a tourist), and therein you have the perfect excuse to get to the beach. All of us who live here, seldom ever even notice that "Big Emerald Thing" sitting south of us. My buddy from Ft. Walton calls me every once in a while and asks me, "How's the surf?" And I never know. I always forget to pause a moment and take a short little stroll to the beach (you remember, that sandy place with the sea oats).

The visitors to our fair villages have a different dilemma: Time on their hands and no direction. They often look as lost as young puppies. They can find the Seaside post office, but have no idea where to find a good cheeseburger. Show them the way to the Seagrove Village Café; just let them know there ain't no parking. It seems like we just have to team up. You, my local friend, can be their savior. When they whine about going to the Red Bar and it's so crowded they can't even get in, tell them about LaLa's Saltwater Grill. Better still, take them there, and make them buy the beer. When they complain about how crowded, and sandy, and wet the beaches are, bite your tongue, count to ten, and then tell them about Pt. Washington and Eden State Park. Tell them to take a boat ride up the Choctawhatchee River.

If a newcomer asks "how's the bike path?" Don't answer, "I dunno, I've never been on it." Just blow the dust off your rusting Huffy and get out there. It's really cool to be a tour guide. Take them to Rosemary Beach or show them the marina at WaterColor. And most importantly, if they are looking for fine dining, and they are paying the bill, tell them Bud and Alley's, Criolla's, or Café 30-A. Live large at their expense. They won't get the bill 'til next month. Don't forget, all you visitors that might be listening, we pay beach prices all the time. That's probably why we're all working too hard. Paradise is expensive. But it's worth it. Let's all just take the time to enjoy it.

PALM TREES

A bit of a hubbub was brewed recently when a local writer was daring enough to critique WaterColor and their decision to plant palm trees in front of their entrance. This was derided, by the author, as hypocritical, and all sorts of things. It was viewed as anti-songbird, etc., etc. My girlfriend was offended by the outrage, and came immediately to WaterColor's defense. She, being from Mississippi, which is (how shall we put it?) "coastline-deprived," put a value on palm trees that was almost spiritual. She pointed out to me, in no uncertain terms, that people coming from Mississippi, and from Alabama, Missouri, Idaho, and on and on, venture down to this coastline, for the Florida experience, which has to include palm trees. For some reason, scrub-oaks were simply OK. (I personally feel that the scrub oak is the most unique and expressive of all major trees, demonstrating a form that is twisted and shaped by years of harsh winds and weather. But I digress.) Palm trees were the essential setting that visitors wished to be immersed in. Jamaica has palm trees, The Bahamas have palm trees, Miami has palm trees. By God, the Panhandle must have palm trees. She doesn't seem to mind the awesome oaks that stand guard on the grounds of Eden. But when she gets near the beach, she must have her palm trees. Magnolias, in their flowered majesty, can be found in every southern state, but Florida has to have its palm trees, even if they aren't really "native." We have to become the "no boat Bahamas," the place within driving distance, that we can all sit back, sip a margarita, gaze out at the emerald waters, and bask in the "tropical vacation land experience." Apparently, to her, this cannot be accomplished without being in the shade of palm trees. Perhaps she's right. The oaks of Eden are very antebellum. The scrub oaks of Eastern Lake and Grayton have a bonsai, almost oriental, feel to them. The magnolias that are scattered everywhere have just too darn many flowers to really be a tropical tree. I guess we should just sit back and embrace the invasion of the palms. And, perhaps, have one more margarita. Chill, mon, chill.

The Old Bridge

I ventured off the asphalt, wearing blue jeans and my hiking boots, in the sweltering late August heat. I was going to blaze a trail through the thick, Florida forest, somewhere in the wilderness of Inlet Beach, in hopes of finding the bayou, several hundred yards to the north. But from my very first steps, I was transported... I felt a feeling I hadn't had in many years, as I felt the crunch of my foot steps on the carpet of deer moss. I don't know how prevalent it is throughout the south, but in the untamed portions of northwest Florida, deer moss is a unique, singular feature that seems to conjure up my childhood, like nothing else. And I was transported back to the days we use to roam the forests north of Eastern Lake. I was probably about eight years old when we took the old jeep trail that crossed the newly completed Highway 30-A. The highway, in those days, was a gravel mixture; not the smooth asphalt that it is today. It consisted of gray gravel embedded in something like crushed concrete. I suppose it was to add better traction, or possibly, just to be cheaper. All the pebbles were gray, but if we looked close, we would find a nugget or two that was a bright golden rust color, and we would keep them, thinking or hoping, they were real gold. Our imagination ran wild, in those days.

Our adventures took us past the highway, headed north, up the lonesome jeep track, and we were headed into no man's land, armed only with our BB guns, and a sturdy walking stick. We never seemed to see much wildlife. There was always a certain barren feeling to a lot of this forest. When we ventured off the trail, we would wind our way around well-spaced pine trees, and feel that familiar crunch of the deer moss. For those unfamiliar to this terrain, deer moss is a lichen or a fungus that covers the forest floor in many places, and it looks just like tiny gray green well-formed bushes. It seems to invite imagination...

In certain places, the barren landscape changed dramatically. The land dipped a bit, and the bushes grew dense and impenetrable, and you suddenly became aware of tall majestic cypress trees with their signature tapering trunks, rising out of small ponds. Their branches added a new, different green canopy in lovely contrast to the ever-present pine branches. You imagined how the animals probably congregated around this pond, when the humans weren't around.

My brothers and I had ventured this old trail a few times before. Each time, we went a little further. One day, we took it all the way to what seemed to be a bit of a ridge, where the slope of the road seemed to climb a tiny bit from the normally flat surroundings, and, after topping the ridge, we saw it!

Before our eyes, in the middle of this forest, at the foot of a slight valley that lay before us, we saw the bridge... we discovered a bridge in the middle of nowhere. It wasn't a working bridge, but just the bare bone remnants of a bridge. But to see the rectangular, orderly patterns of some old man-made construction, in the middle of the woods, was amazing. There were many pilings still standing in line, and enough of the beams were still holding their places in the noble construction that we were able to carefully make our way across it, and gaze down into the black water stream below it, the headwaters of Eastern Lake.

It was surely an old bridge. One line of beams was mostly fallen in. The other one was somewhat intact, with maybe a few beams, laying with one end still in place, and the other resting in the mud, waiting someday to be swallowed by the swamp. There was no planking left, to speak of; just the slight, straight, hollowed out forms of withered wood, here and there, clinging to the huge, rusty nails that stood defiant in rows, where the boards they once held tight had fallen away into the water.

I saw a piece of an old, white, porcelain coffee cup, lying serenely at the bottom of the shallow stream, and I just knew, as a boy of eight years old, that that coffee cup once belonged to a Confederate cavalry lieutenant, and I could see the troop of rebel horsemen riding intently across that once proud bridge. Of course, I knew it was just my imagination. I knew the Civil War never really ventured into this forbidding territory. But, I could feel the nobility and the strength of character it had taken for some good strong men to haul the timber down that long dirt road from the Wesley lumber mill, at Point Washington, and place them in sturdy formation, for a generation or two of our ancestors to make their way to the natural paradise of Eastern Lake.

THE CHRISTMAS TREE

Hampton gazed out the window at the cedar tree that gently curved around the old Florida cottage. It was the week before Christmas and he had driven through a thunderstorm to Ft. Walton and back, to buy one last Christmas card, and now he lay tired in his bed, cuddled with only his comforting blanket. The tree was all a pattern of lights that calmly twinkled in the cold dark night, and he was amazed. In his half sleep-filled thoughts, the tree looked so much like a Christmas tree, the tiny lights fading rhythmically in and out, like a thousand fireflies. The dancing tiny lights, however, didn't fly about, and Hamp was puzzled...his mind happily humming at half speed. Did the neighbors sneak in late in the afternoon and decorate the tree while he was gone? The grand, gracefully bent, ancient tree clearly grew from their side of the imaginary property line to frame Hamp's side of the western sky. Hampton quietly grinned at himself...you sleepy fool, the lights were tiny raindrops left captured in the uniform brush-like leaves of the cedar. They assumed a random "orderliness" that just seemed to mimic the array of tiny white Christmas tree lights. The light was thousands of miniature raindrops portraying prisms from the light of a neighboring streetlight. No matter that Hampton's sleepy mind mistook it for a string of electrical bulbs, the reality was even better. It was a true, natural, living Christmas tree with all the beautiful light, peace and tranquility shared on this most gentle of winter nights.

The Pirate Ship

My man-cave is a Pirate Ship. The place of peace and tranquility, that I go to, in my hour of need, is a structure of old planks and boards, many of which were once flotsam from a hurricane. I pieced them together thru the years, just because.

The history of the Pirate Ship started in the aftermath of Hurricane Dennis. After most major storms, such as Opal, Ivan, and Dennis, an enormous debris field is usually deposited on my lakeshore. With Dennis having the highest storm surge on record for the last 30 years, the amount of flotsam and jetsam that we accumulated was immense. There is no human way to clear all this debris by hand. It was a tangled mess of straw, weeds and lumber from battered dune walkovers, and everything else that had been floating on the seas for years. Fortunately, I was able to pull a few good boards out of the mess before the county came in with bulldozers to collect the rest. I had a modest stack of 6x6's and a few 2x8's and 2x12's. Nothing special, but I kept them stacked neatly, for some reason.

Finally, one day, I decided we had to have a cabana of some sort, down near the lake. It has been an ongoing family tradition to build some kind of modest decks, some of which grew to be full scale shacks, and then, of course, it has been tradition for hurricanes to come and reduce these shacks to rubble. But, it is simply necessary to have a sitting place by such a lovely scene, and one day I sank a few rustic, salvaged, 6x6's in the ground, and began my structure. This time I placed it up nestled in the line of scrub oaks, a half dozen feet above the water line of the lake. It would be safe there, I supposed.

I had no plan, really. I installed the 6x6's in a square, with beams above, picturing a small hipped roof, above, later on. I ran the old, salvaged 2x12 and 2x8 deck boards long out the front, and was contemplating, perhaps, a semi-circular cantilevered entrance deck to the small square cabana. About this time, in the slow casual process of this thing, my wife, Nina, came to inspect my progress one day. We had recently heard the great news that our son, Chris, and his wife, Kristin, were expecting our first grandson, who would be named

Beckett. After seeing the basic rough structure I had pieced together so far, she seemed to have a vision, as she, actually, bent down on one knee, and brought her arms up, in the classic "rifleman" gesture, as we all did as kids, and exclaimed, "This can be a Fort, where Beckett fights off the Pirates..."

Well, a light bulb went off, in my head. Not a small light bulb. A gigantic light bulb went off, and I knew in an instant, that this structure was going to be a Pirate Ship.

That was the easy part: the inspiration that came from my wife. The hard part was to build the thing; to bend the boards and to envision the curves and the sweeps that would come together to fulfill this dream. But, it really wasn't physically hard, since there really was no timeline, no set completion date. It was simply something I could tinker with, on weekends, and add a nuance or two, here and there. But I always knew I could do it; I could figure out any problem. And I always knew it would bring a smile to most anyone who saw it.

Shortly after I fashioned the curved basic hull shape of the "boat", I knew I had to have an operable gang plank, to board the boat, and to pull up, to stay safe from the pirates. I made it, by trial and error, where it could be lifted by ropes and pulleys. This gang plank rested on a dock, all on dry land, of course, but it soon dawned on me, that it was simply mandatory that the gangplank pass over water. This, of course, led me to install a small pond beneath the gangplank. Fine and dandy, as they say, but this pond soon became rank and fowl, since it was simply stagnant water. This problem, of course, only had one solution: I would have to build a waterfall, to keep the water moving. This " improvement" to the over-all scheme only took a moment of inspiration, of course, but took many, many long hours of hard work, with me enlisting many of my friends and family to carry landscaping rocks and mortar, down to the lakeside. You can research "how to build a waterfall" with just a couple taps on the computer. How to do it, in real life, is just plain hard work, but immensely satisfying.

This highlights, really, what was one of my main motivations, and possibly a profound life lesson, as well. This whole endeavor can kind of be encapsulated by that old saying "painting yourself into a corner," but on a much grander scale. Once I actually got some of the early shape and structure of the pirate ship, and got grins of joy, from people who saw it, I knew that I would have to keep fixing it up. After doing each portion, and then sitting back with a beer, just contemplating what I had done, I just keep thinking of more things I could do to it. For instance, somewhere, in the back of my mind, I knew I would have to have a mast, but then that led to having rope rigging, and that would lead to inventing just how to do that. There was no manual on the internet for that. For instance, it started out open-aired, with just a square beam system above, but I realized that I should probably put a ceiling over it. Then I realized the ceiling could be a "second floor," as well, and then the second floor changed into a "crow's nest," complete with oblong railing, and a crooked ship's ladder. If there is anything I have learned from this experience of imagination, it is the old saying, "one thing leads to another..." When the light bulb went off, in all its momentary brilliance, it filled me with imagination, and it also sealed my fate that I would have to see this through to "completion," whatever that meant.

Another revelation came to me on another day, as I was trying to finish varnishing the floor of the crow's nest. Here I was sweating profusely, getting icky with the varnish all over me, and cursing how much hard, hard work I had put into this crazy endeavor, this dream of mine. In the back of my mind, I think I always knew that what I was trying to do was to build my own version of "The Swiss Family Robinson House", the incredible treehouse of my youth. And it dawned on me, in a somewhat dimmer lightbulb than before, that the Swiss Family Robinson didn't actually build that treehouse; the Walt Disney Corporation, with teams of production designers, and engineers, and teams of expert carpenters built that treehouse!

It dawned on me, as I varnished that last patch of cedar flooring on the crow's nest of my Pirate Ship, that I had been pursuing a dream, far beyond my capabilities, but that, through my persistent naiveté, my innate and acquired skills, and just my perspiring perseverance, I had accomplished it.

And now it is my fortress of solitude, where I contemplate the winds and the seas... and all is peaceful, on my Pirate Ship.

The Seagrove Village Market

It was in the summer of 2001, that a chance encounter at the Seagrove Village Market would change my life. I was a bachelor, in those days, living alone in a camper trailer, as I built my house on Eastern Lake. I usually didn't eat breakfast during weekdays, but every Saturday morning, I had a ritual where I went to the Seagrove Village Market Café and treated myself to breakfast. Not only did I order the same Mexican omelet, with hash browns, orange juice, and coffee, every Saturday morning, but I always sat at the same corner booth, and saw the same two or three Seagrove denizens, all sitting at the same booths that they always sat in, every Saturday morning. It was beginning to feel like an episode of the Twilight Zone.

For some unknown reason that I simply can't explain, I found myself going into the Seagrove Village Market on a Thursday morning. I sat down at my standard corner booth. I ordered and ate my standard breakfast, and was finishing my coffee, when I noticed a good-looking woman come in, and sit down at a nearby booth, across the room. Having lived in Seagrove since the pre-Seaside era, I could tell, at a glance, she wasn't from around here. She had her hair pinned up in an elegant way. She had a purple Chico, California t-shirt on, and I thought for a moment she must be from Destin.

I'm not sure if I was able to catch her looking my way, and even if I did, I'm not sure what I would have done about it. I noticed she was talking with the waitress, Rachel Merideth, who was an old friend of mine, and, before I had a chance to be shy and undecided, Rachel turned and introduced me to Nina McCaslin, from Jackson, Mississippi. Perhaps I was still too sleepy to realize that normally I'm a fairly shy individual, but suddenly I found myself asking her if I could join her for a cup of coffee.

I sat down and we began to talk. I soon found out that she was a contractor, and, not only was I impressed, but I realized, right away, that we had a lot in common. I found out, soon thereafter, that, not only was she beautiful on the outside, but she had a great sense of humor, and a joyous laughter that was just simply heartwarming. I was probably smitten from that morning for ever after, but it took me a couple of years of dating Nina to realize that she was the most kind and loving woman I would ever know, and that I would be forever honored to have her as my wife.

As we approach the tenth anniversary of our marriage, I realize that the woman I married is even better than I could have ever asked for, and I owe God a great debt of gratitude for bringing us together at the Seagrove Village Market.

MISSISSIPPI MUD

I looked at my shoes. I had just gotten into the nice, white car, and I had mud on my nice, black, patent leather shoes. These were my "dress up" shoes; the ones I wore to cosmopolitan dinners and real estate functions, and the ones I wore to funerals. This time it was for a funeral. They now had mud caked a little bit up the sides. It was mud, alright, but is was Mississippi mud.

And I have to thank my wife for that. I have to thank my wife for being from Mississippi. I have to thank my wife for introducing me to her family, time and time again, and I just love it. I feel connected to the people in the Delta, and I feel connected to the folks in Jackson. I know what family is, and where they come from. People in Mississippi know each other, and there is a certain connection with your neighbor that I haven't quite experienced in my state. I settled in Florida, after a rambling childhood. I haven't got a clue what it means to have cousins, dear and close to you, for over forty years or more, but I'm learning, from my wife.

And now, I have mud on my shoes, Mississippi mud, because I walked out on a soggy, small cemetery behind a white, peacefully elegant, old clapboard country church, and I read the tombstones, that carried the same proud names, and I huddled with a bunch of magnificent strangers, gathered in love for a recently loved one, somehow departed. She was my wife's cousin, and I sensed how wonderful she was, by how wonderful my wife is, and how wonderful this group of solemn, sweet strangers is. We might not have anything in common, or, most likely, never see each other again, but for this wondrous, soggy, solemn moment we all shared the gratitude and the grace, of the Mississippi mud.

WHEN I'M SIXTY-FOUR

Time is most definitely like a river. It is sweet and calm as it comes from its head waters, it is smooth and even, as it undulates through the middle of your life. And, honestly, it gets a bit more hectic, and faster, as you approach the rapids, and the waterfall...

I will take you back to 1967. There's this band, called The Beatles, who have somehow elevated their evolution, in a leap of faith called Sgt. Pepper's Lonely Heart's Club Band. It is an extremely diverse album, with styles and textures that range the gamut of popular music. It is no longer rock and roll. It isn't just sweet psychedelic scenes. It isn't just ruminations of the meaning, or lack of meaning, of life. It is life, in chapters hauntingly familiar to us all. I was about sixteen years old when I first heard the words "in a boat on a river with tangerine trees and marmalade skies." I was sixteen, or perhaps, I was "just seventeen," but these images had an impact. They pushed open a door to my imagination and I walked through that door into that whole wide new world.

There was another song or two on that album, not as prominent as the well-known classics, that had subtle beautiful tunes, none the less. "She's Leaving Home" can't possibly have come from a rock and roll band... the sublime melodies carried through with violins and cello...the counterpoint harmonies of Paul and John, exquisite in their melancholy...and, remember, this was possibly the most overlooked song on this entire album. And then there is the tune, "When I'm Sixty-Four." It's just a ditty. And I cannot deny that the Beatles created a whole lot of ditties; small pieces of melody and whimsy, words and rhythm, intertwined with a story and a backbeat, but his one particular song, written by a British boy in his twenties, and included on, possibly, the greatest album of all time, is pertaining to me today.

You see, I am now, today, sixty-four. And I can look across the kitchen table, at the woman I love, and all the questions of that young man's lyrics, are all answered in her eyes. "Will you still need me, will you still feed me, when I'm sixty-four?" Of course, the answer is yes, and, of course, the answer is reflected in both of us. And, is just feels good that we seem to be living inside a Beatles song.

ALYS BEACH

Cruising down highway 30-A, in this vast new millennium we have entered, in the wavering heat of a summer afternoon, it appears rather abruptly, somewhat like a mirage... These days, quite oddly enough, a lot of the beloved highway we travel on has become much too much like a desert; a desert of ordinary buildings, a desert of repetitious houses and condos that duplicate a formula of sorts. They may be different colors, different shapes, and different textures, but there can get to be a tedious uniformity to the practicalities of these beach communities that starts to make it all seem like a wood clad concrete desert.

And then you arrive at Alys Beach, where an oasis of architecture envelopes you, as if a sudden, cool sea breeze has just kissed you in the face. The vistas that unfold before your eyes are like the taste of cold, clear water to the lips of your soul. Tall, pristine parapets rise in elegant, muted curves. The pure, distilled whiteness of it all invokes the timelessness of the crystal white sands these houses seem to honor.

The avenues are inviting. As you venture afoot, natural stone lends a ruggedness to your journey, only to be contrasted against the stark white perfect walls, and the huge elegant shapes of pottery that seem to punctuate every entranceway. The shutters and doors are carved from ancient, precious, well-worn lumber, stained in playful hews as comforting contrast against the constant white. Is this a taste of Bermuda? An insinuation of Morocco? Or is this something even more unfamiliar in its allure...

You venture northeast. An array of precision towers beckons you to explore. Before your eyes, there seems to be a perimeter enforced by walls, perhaps enclosing a secret courtyard. But then you find the gate, and venture past the pillars that stand as sentry, and it unfolds before you...

The Pool is truly the core of this oasis. It is the primal pond so sacred in this garden, this cultured jungle. It is the watering hole for the brown skinned natives, so sleek and elegant, as they lounge beside the Pool. The breeze is strong and vibrant from the ocean in the distance. The palm trees bow gently in proud servitude. They maintain your shade. They comfort every inch of your body, as you let your stresses dissolve into sky.

You wade in slowly, but the salt like water isn't cold or disturbing. It isn't warm either. It's neutral, and inviting. You seem balanced, like you have never been before. An attendant, tall and tan, and smiling, brings you a beverage that suits you like nectar. And all is so very perfect, in the Pool.

Someone brings you a soft towel, and finds your sandals. You depart with a sense of serenity unmatched. It's getting late into the afternoon. The sky turns orange, red, lavender, purple. Clouds intrude with such subtlety they only enhance the glow, and then you watch the sun slip slowly into the sea, after your perfect day at Alys Beach.

TREASURES

There is treasure in the sand dunes south and west of WaterSound. It's not doubloons or pieces-of-eight. It's more a treasure of nature, of vast landscapes of sand and scrub oaks, and miles and miles of blue sky and emerald waters. The gold comes from the sun as it covers you in warmth on a cool autumn day. You can walk for hours on the beach and just drink in the gorgeous breeze. The pristine sand squeaks beneath your feet, the birds squawk in the distant. You try to sneak up on a sandpiper, and you know those tiny little toothpick legs are too quick for you. Humans are almost too big for this environment. You have to reduce yourself, and become one more tiny portion of a vast, beautiful canvas of color and solitude. You find yourself whispering in awe, when your heart wishes to sing. You mustn't leave a fragment of your belongings, merely your footprints in the changing sand. If the wind picks up and it seems to get a little nippy, simply lay a blanket tucked leeward of a giant sand dune, and it's still summertime, even in November. You can climb the highest dunes, picking a path between the nettles and the sea oats, and calmly sit until the sunset. The dolphins sometimes get curious, and bubble up to the surface, perchance to get a glimpse of us in our world. I think sometimes they smile and wink at us and let us all remember it's all so wonderful.

There really is buried treasure, pieces of the past strewn through the sand by countless storms. Fragments of Indian pottery and sometimes, perhaps, an arrowhead will be uncovered by a midnight thunderstorm and lay uncovered for days in just the right spot for you to fortune upon, if it's your lucky day. If not, the pieces will always still be there sheltered beneath the sand and you will still be very lucky to have walked this precious beach.

THE END OF THE BEGINNING

I guess I'm new at writing a book. Even if it's a book about something old. It's common knowledge that a book should have a theme, but I started out without one. But then a theme emerged, somewhere between the commas and the periods. Between the photographs and prose. Between the fifties and the 'teens. The theme emerged as two separate sources, much like the springs and gentle rainfall, that constantly nourish the coastal dune lakes. The restless sands of shifting ocean shorelines form a berm, at first, that hugs the softly rising waters, in a strong and sheltering embrace, then gives way, finally, when the reservoir surpasses its earthly bounds, and the lake swiftly emerges into the vast awaiting ocean. The theme is two things: constancy and change, the time we dwell in calm serenity, gathering a thousand thoughts, sometimes like gentle rains, sometimes like lightning storms, and it fills us to the brink of our capacity, and we are sitting like a vast, clear mirror smooth lake, and yet a constant pressure builds, with all the forces of wind and gravity, and yet we remain contained, and constant, until the change...

And something sparks the change, something as subtle as the kiss of a morning rain, or something as violent as the tropics in turmoil. The change can start as gently as a heron's glide, but soon can obtain the velocity of an osprey diving for its prey. The calm, silent lake no longer sits in contemplation, but loses its grip to the inevitability of gravity. It pours forth hard against that berm that once held it in shelter, and the berm, once compact and mighty, slowly crumbles, piece by piece, and merges into the stream. The swirling is the merger of two forces, the constancy of the sand being eaten by the inevitable change of rushing water. It's a dance that has carried on since the beginning of time. And then, slowly, weeks or months from now, the ocean, with its waves of change, gives new weight and constancy to the sand. It reconstitutes its compact barrier. It caresses the arms of the lake in a new sheltering embrace, the lake rebuilds its reservoir of strength and serenity, with every summer rain, and then the dance begins again.

65846193R00068

Made in the USA
Charleston, SC
04 January 2017